CAVAN
FOLK
TALES

CAVAN
FOLK
TALES

GARY BRANIGAN

The
History
Press
Ireland

Dedicated to Jeannette, Tara, Aoife, and Rory

First published 2016

The History Press Ireland
50 City Quay
Dublin 2
Ireland
www.thehistorypress.ie

The History Press Ireland is a member of Publishing Ireland,
the Irish Book Publisher's Association.

© Gary Branigan, 2016
Illustrations © Elena Danaan, 2016

The right of Gary Branigan to be identified as the author
of this work has been asserted in accordance with the
Copyrights, Designs and Patents Act 1988.

British Library Cataloguing in Publication Data.
A catalogue record for this book is available from the British Library.

ISBN 978 1 84588 229 7

Typesetting and origination by The History Press

CONTENTS

ACKNOWLEDGEMENTS

So much has been written of the rich indigenous culture extant in our fair isle. From language, custom, dress, music, and folklore, the island peoples on the western fringes of Europe are celebrated for their unique way of life.

Within Ireland, many localities have their own idiosyncrasies and home-grown customs, stories, and lore, borne out of local history and local circumstance.

The lakeland county of Cavan is no exception, and this book was created with the intention of sharing and celebrating some of its wealth of local stories and lore.

Many of these stories are old and have been handed down through generations whilst others are more modern, showing the continuance of the Irish traditions of the *seanchaí* and of Irish storytelling. In reading through the various tales gathered here, the reader will be transported to a former time and place of yore, long gone, but forever preserved.

I would like to express my sincere gratitude to the many people, past and present, for the kind assistance, guidance, and encouragement received, both directly and indirectly, during the compilation of this book.

Research facilities at the National Library of Ireland, Ulster Folk and Transport Museum in Holywood, Cavan County Museum,

National Museum of Ireland (Country Life), Royal Society of Antiquaries of Ireland, Office of Public Works, Ordnance Survey Ireland, UCD, and the various local historical, folkloric and heritage societies have all been invaluable, and thanks go to the wonderful staff who maintain them.

Special mention deserves to go to Críostóir Mac Cárthaigh of the National Folklore Collection at UCD; to local storyteller Ali Isaac for inspiring so many aspiring storytellers; to John Middleton and James Mathews, for editing and proofreading; to Maureen Slough, John Boylan, and Stephen McEntee for local guidance and valuable advice: to Ronan Colgan and Beth Amphlett of The History Press Ireland for their endless patience and for ongoing assistance during the publication process; and to Elena Danaan of Awen's Gift Creations, who created the absolutely amazing images for the book, and to whom I owe a significant debt of gratitude.

Thanks also to the many others – too many to mention here – who assisted in various ways in bringing this book to completion.

Finally, words alone cannot express my sincere gratitude and appreciation to Jeannette, Tara, Aoife and Rory, for the love, support, encouragement and patience they have shown throughout this journey.

Gary Branigan
Cavan, 2016

INTRODUCTION

My contribution to this collection of folk tales is in my capacity as a storyteller, and, for the most part, not as an academic or historian. Fact and fable are inextricably woven into the fabric of the Irish gene, and it is not always possible to separate them. However, I have attempted to be as faithful as I can to both.

The medium of telling stories and singing songs is the way the Irish have been able to come to terms with fortune and misfortune alike. Many of the stories collected here have been handed down from generation to generation, by local people for local people; others are more modern. In both cases, it is my hope and belief that anybody will be able to pick up this book and easily enjoy the rich bounty of Cavan's storytelling tradition. In selecting tales for inclusion in this publication, I have tried my best to include a range generally representative of the county as a whole.

Cavan, affectionately known as 'The Lakeland County' and 'The Breffni', is one of the three border counties within the province of Ulster that is located in the Republic of Ireland. Covering some 730 square miles of rugged and scenic terrain with its beautiful 365 lakes, County Cavan has a current and growing population of circa 75,000. The majority of the county is sparsely populated, with many of its people residing in larger towns of Bailieboro, Belturbet, Cootehill, Kingscourt, and Cavan town.

The county is characterised by drumlin countryside dotted with many rivers, lakes, and hills, with the highest point being Cuilcagh Mountain, at 2,182ft high. The source of many rivers can be found in the county, among them the rivers Erne, Blackwater, and of course the mighty Shannon, which emerges from the darkness of the mysterious Shannon Pot.

Derived from the Irish *An Cabhán*, meaning 'The Hollow', Cavan possesses a rich tapestry of history, legend, and folklore. From the earliest times of Fionn MacCumhaill to the monastic influences of St Cillian and St Feidhlim, from the medieval battles for control of the East Bréifne kingdom to the mass displacement of the natives through forced plantation and avoidable famine, Cavan has had more than its fair share of significant events over the millennia. It is central to many of Ireland's most famous and fantastic myths and legends.

1

HISTORY

BISHOP BEDELL AND THE TEMPLEPORT BIBLE

The Rt Revd William Bedell was an Anglican churchman who served as Lord Bishop of Kilmore. He was martyred during the Irish Rebellion of 1641, during the time of the Reformation. Born at Black Notley in Essex, Bedell was educated at Emmanuel College in Cambridge, where he became a fellow and subsequently took orders.

In 1607, he was appointed chaplain to Sir Henry Wotton, then English ambassador at Venice, where he remained for four years, acquiring a great reputation as a scholar, theologian, printer, and missionary to the faithful living under Roman Catholic tyranny of the Inquisition.

In 1627, because of his ceaseless efforts for nationalist evangelism, he was appointed provost of Trinity College, Dublin, despite having no prior connection with Ireland. Thus, he was at the forefront of advancing the Irish Reformation when he decreed that the church services, including the New Testament, be read in the Irish language so that the monoglot masses might understand their messages in contrast with the Catholic method of reading in Latin to a clueless congregation.

In 1629, he was appointed to become Bishop of Kilmore and Ardagh, and set out to reform the abuses of his diocese, which had been notorious for its corruption and bribery. Additionally, to further promote literacy and religious enlightenment, he encouraged the use of the Irish language in all aspects of ecclesiastical affairs, and personally undertook the duties generally discharged by the bishop's lay chancellor. He also appointed only Irish speakers to parishes to further his mission to the common folk.

Bedell is noted for commissioning the translation of the Bible into the Irish language, the translation of which was undertaken by the Protestant Rector of Templeport parish, the Revd Muircheartach Ó Cionga.

Bedell was a man of simple life, often walking miles on foot or on horse, travelling the dangerous byways. This was a particularly dangerous period as Irish Catholic nobles and leaders who adhered to ancient privileges of the chieftainship had made common cause with Catholic powers in Europe in causing treason, sabotage, and general warfare. Indeed, Bedell made a point of entering anti-Protestant and especially anti-English areas, encouraging and providing assistance to converts to Protestantism, including supporting them whilst studying for the ministry.

Bedell was also noted for his even application of the law in prosecuting the guilty and providing help against corruption, regardless of a person's religious adherence. For instance, he sided with the Catholics of Kilmore against the excess of Alan Cooke, the incumbent chancellor of the diocese. However, the Church courts found that Cooke had legally acquired the right as chancellor and the bishop was unable to remove him.

However, because of his support within the common Irish, especially the Catholic Irish leadership fearful of his standing, Bedell was considered a high-value target by Irish Catholic rebels. With the outbreak of the Irish Rebellion of 1641, the local warlords, led by the O'Reillys, took control of the area. Nonetheless, whilst support for the rebellion had yet to bear full fruit, the rebel leadership trod carefully around the popular bishop. Thus, the O'Reillys 'gave comfortable words to the Bishop' and Bedell's house at Kilmore in County Cavan was left untouched.

Indeed, because of Bishop Bedell's popularity among Catholic and Protestants alike, not only did Protestant Irish refugees flock to him; he also appealed to Catholics who were unwilling to join the rebellion. As the rebellion grew increasingly bloody and entire Protestant families were murdered, Bedell's property became a place of refuge for hundreds of families from the area seeking shelter from the rebel insurgents.

In the end, however, the rebels insisted upon the immediate release into their capture of all who had taken shelter in his house. Knowing full well that they would likely be mass murdered, the bishop refused. Having isolated the bishop and the refugees, the rebels believed they could murder the bishop and refugees in silence. They mounted an assault, seized Bedell and other known missionaries of the Reformation, and imprisoned them on the nearby island castle of Lough Oughter, Cloughoughter Castle.

Here, Bedell and others were imprisoned for several weeks and tortured. When the rebellion began to subside, his captors, fearing for their own safety, forced him into signing a deposition and a remonstrance from his captors, 'pleading on their behalf for graces from King Charles'. Freed, Bedell was now released into the care of his friend Denis Sheridan but the imprisonment and torture had worked their damage. Shortly after his release, Bedell died from his wounds and exposure on 7 February 1642.

Bishop Bedell was afforded the dignity by his captors of being buried next to his wife Leah at Kilmore, where he received an honourable funeral in the presence of his O'Raghallaigh (O'Reilly) captors. At his funeral, a Roman Catholic priest, Father Farrelly, was heard to say, 'May my soul be with Beddell's'.

THE MAXWELLS OF FARNHAM

There are few families in more modern times that have had more influence on the county than the religious and stately Maxwell family.

Approximately 2 miles from the county town is the present-day Radisson Blu Farnham Estate Hotel, with its fine old house and accompanying lakes, wooded areas, and open pasture lands. In former times, this plush pad was the residence of the Maxwell family ever since their arrival from Lanarkshire, Scotland, way back in 1664, during the time of the plantations.

With their family motto of '*Je suit prêt*', meaning 'I am ready', they soon built a fine estate by improving the local landscape and the look of the estate grounds and local areas. Unlike many others of the planted ascendancy, they also saw it as part of their lot to give the tenants that lived within the borders of their estate a better shot at life. They employed various inspectors, whose job it was to report on and recommend improvements to the diet, living conditions,and education of those resident there.

The Maxwells were fervently religious and employed 'moral agents' who kept an eye on the locals to make sure that they were behaving themselves and not indulging in unsuitable activities. This was a big catch to receiving their charity. Among other things, the tenantry were bound to observe the Lord's Day, refrain from cursing, and not involve themselves in the distillation or consumption of alcohol. We can only imagine it was a bundle of laughs living there at that time.

The fine grounds of Farnham drew many admirers, with one young topographer in the nineteenth century saying that it was 'one of the finest places that I have ever seen in Ireland'. He also declared that the lakes within the estate were 'uncommonly beautiful; extensive and have a shore extremely varied'.

Sadly, the Lord and Lady Farnham were killed in the Abergele train disaster in 1868. The tenants erected a statue in his honour in Cavan town, which now stands in front of the new Johnston Library. They deemed it fit not to erect a statue of the good Lady – more's the pity.

FROM QUILCA TO LILLIPUT

The Dean of St Patrick's Cathedral in Dublin, Jonathan Swift, was an ambitious and accomplished man, if not a bit of a strange fish. He was an unusual man of his day and, having being raised by his uncle, had an unusual outlook on life and the world that he saw. He is generally regarded as being the greatest satirist who ever wrote in the English language, often bitter and delightfully humorous in equal measure.

Whilst staying with his friend Revd Thomas Sheridan in Quilca House, near the present-day Mullagh village, in the early seventeenth century, he worked on two of his major works, *Tale of a Tub*, and the much more well-known *Gulliver's Travels*.

Despite being a very welcome guest of the Sheridans and waited on hand, foot and finger, he composed a poem whilst he was there showing that he was not a particularly gracious and appreciative gent.

To Quilca, a Country House not in Good Repair

Let me thy Properties explain,
A rotten Cabin, dropping Rain;

Chimnies with Scorn rejecting Smoak;
Stools, Tables, Chairs, and Bed-steds broke:
Here Elements have lost their Vses,
Air ripens not, nor Earth produces:
In vain we make poor *Sheelah* toil,
Fire will not roast, nor Water boil.
Thro' all the Vallies, Hills, and Plains,
The Goddess *Want* in Triumph reigns;
And her chief Officers of State,
Sloth, *Dirt*, and *Theft* around her wait.

THE LAST HIGHWAYMAN

In the days of the highwaymen, a chief robber by the name of 'Captain' Mooney had his quarters in amongst the trees of an old man-made island lair on Lough Ramor, not far from the town of Virginia. He, of course, was not a real captain but this was a title bestowed upon him by the local people, who held him in such high esteem.

The captain is said to have been tough and fearless but kind and just in all his dealings with every man and woman whose path he crossed. He discharged his duties with the utmost diligence and care, and those duties were to guarantee the provision of the poor people in the district as only a highwayman can.

Mooney's territory covered many of the approach roads to the town, and both he and his men would camouflage themselves, hide amongst the gorse and brambles and lie in wait for a passing carriage. When a vehicle belonging to someone possessing a certain level of wealth – usually a landlord or rich gent – did eventually pass, he and his men would jump out and seize it at gunpoint and relieve the passengers of their possessions.

When he got back to his lair on the *crannóg*, he divided up the spoils to share with the poor and distressed of the parish. If a poor person in the district was in need of anything, they would go to Captain Mooney and he would make sure that they were given what they needed; it was for this reason that he was loved by the poor.

In those days there was no police, and it was the men of His Majesty's Revenue who carried out the same duties. The revenue men, acting on the orders of the wealthy, offered a reward of £100 to anybody who would provide information leading to the capture of the captain.

On a particularly dark and blustery night, Captain Mooney and a companion lay in wait for an unsuspecting traveller, as they had done before on many an occasion. When a suitable target came by Mooney and his man jumped out, forced the carriage to a halt and robbed the old rich man inside, who was a gent by the name of Burke. The revenue men just happened to be in the vicinity at the time and heard the screams of the man, so blew their whistles and gave immediate chase to the men, tracking them by their muddy boot prints all along the way.

In a bid to escape, the men found themselves forced to wade through the Blackwater River at the ferry house, and it was here that the revenue men caught up with them. They were thigh high in the water when the officers fired a shot at them, hitting Mooney's companion in the arm, and making him lose his footing. He was carried down the river and into the lake by the water's current. He was not heard from ever again and it can only be assumed that he sank to the muddy depths of Lough Ramor.

The captain continued across the river, discarding his loot on the way to make his pockets lighter. He kept going as fast as he could but unfortunately for him, he got his foot caught in an eel trap set at the bottom of the river and fell into the water. The revenue men chose to take the man alive and brought him to the local barracks for to be incarcerated pending his trial. They could not believe their luck in securing the capture of the Captain Mooney.

The following day, he was brought to Cavan town for his trial and the Justice of the Peace deemed it necessary to sentence him to penal servitude in Van Diemen's Land; it was here that he ended his days.

There had not been another highwayman in the locality since that time.

THE GREAT HUNGER AND THE UNION WORKHOUSE

There were very bad times in Ireland long ago. It was over 150 years ago now when the vicious blight travelled over on the warm air from Europe and afflicted the potatoes in the ground, causing them to turn black and rotten.

The people all over the island only had small plots of land from which to feed their families and the only thing they had to grow were lumper potatoes. The disease afflicted the lumper the worst and the people were left with nothing to eat, practically overnight.

It wasn't long before the people started to die of starvation, and the heavy odour of rotten spuds and death settled over the land. People were dying so quickly that they could not make coffins fast enough, and there are even stories of people being buried alive. There is one particular story of a man who was being placed into a grave when he awoke, saying, 'Do not bury me for I am not yet dead.' The doctor at the graveside, who had lost his mind through sheer exhaustion, said, 'You are a liar! The doctor knows best,' and the trench was filled in.

Out of desperation, the poor people tried to sow the rotten potatoes the next year in the hope of getting a crop, but nothing grew, and many were so desperate that they ate the grass in the hope of getting some sustenance. There were twice as many people living in Ireland then as there are now, as many have since left this life or this land for places better.

Many of those who stayed used to leave their houses in the mornings and go around from place to place looking for something, anything, to eat. Many still ended up in the union workhouses. These workhouses were places set up to look after those who could not look after themselves, and many workhouses were horrid places, full of desperate people in desperate situations.

One day, a man named Jimmy was tending to his wife Mary at home; seeing that she was quickly fading away through lack of nourishment, the realisation came over him that she was in need of admission to the workhouse in nearby Bawnboy. He thought to himself 'For surely, as bad as life is outside the great walls of the workhouse, life would be a *crumpeen* better inside.' He lifted Mary on to the back of their cart and, seeing as they sold their donkey long previous for provisions, he had to fasten the harness around himself and pull the cart with herself onboard the 5-mile trip all the way to the workhouse.

Pulling the cart was no mean feat for Jimmy given his also weak state of health. He arrived at the workhouse with his back nearly broken just as the sun was setting. He spoke with the mean-spirited superintendent, who berated him for turning up at such an ungodly hour. 'So much for charity,' he thought to himself. Poor Jimmy and Mary were left to sleep out in their cart under the rain with only a woollen blanket to shield them from the elements.

The next morning, they awoke to the sound of the birds singing and the inmates of the workhouse toiling in the fields.

They arose in their damp, mould-ridden clothes and met with the superintendent and the resident priest, Father Doyle.

The two officials sat them down and harshly interrogated them about Mary's background and why they should let her in. Eventually, they grudgingly agreed to admit the poor creature and, upon giving Mary her uniform, directed her to the infirmary where she would be treated.

Jimmy returned home and prayed that poor Mary would recover but when he rose the next day, he had a visit from the neighbour. 'I'm sorry for your loss, a Shéamais,' said he.

'What are you talking about?' replied Jimmy. The neighbour told Jimmy that he had heard of poor Mary's passing in the workhouse. Dropping his rosary beads, Jimmy ran over the hill as fast as he could until he reached the workhouse. 'Where is my Mary? I hear she is dead!' said he to Father Doyle.

'That cannot be, for I only gave her Holy Communion earlier this morning in the infirmary, so I did.'

They rushed to the infirmary to find her bed empty, and the doctor who informed them both that 'It was not that Mary who died at all, but another.' He turned to see the corpse of 'the other Mary' still in her bed and, realising what had happened, all three rushed out to the burial ground and dug the freshly piled earth with their bare hands.

They got down to her shroud and Mary let out a gasp of air. Father Doyle lifted her into the infirmary and after a few days poor Mary recovered. She regained her strength after some weeks and left with her Jimmy for Australia.

BONFIRE OF THE BLACK AND TANS

2016 is the centenary of the great rebellion that took place in the capital and around the country, where proud Irishmen and Irishwomen took up arms against the Crown to protect our own and take back what is, and always was, Irish.

The British Crown forces set up and sent over a new battalion of men who came to be known as the Black and Tans. In reality, they were no more soldiers than ruffians are.

A man named Mahaffey owned a very prosperous business in the local town, situated right in the centre. It was a very large shop that included grocery, drapery, boots, shoes, and hardware. In fact, so large was the premises that there were between twenty and twenty-five hands constantly employed by Mahaffey. Like most young men in the country at the time, the assistants at this shop openly sympathised with the Irish movement for freedom.

A number of days previous, a troop of the Royal Irish Constabulary were ambushed on the back roads with the inspector being shot dead and the others being injured.

The Black and Tans came into the town one evening shortly after and maliciously set fire to the thatch roof, not concerning themselves if there was anybody inside or for the loss of property.

The whole building and stock on the premises at the time were consumed in the conflagration, but luckily those Crown-appointed cowards did not get the satisfaction of killing anybody on this occasion, as the burning was anticipated and precautions had been taken.

This is only one incident of many such events caused by the thuggish Tans.

BEAUFIGHTER PLANE CRASH ON
ST MOGUE'S ISLAND

The wee island birthplace of St Mogue has been used as a burial ground for hundreds if not thousands of years. It is no bigger than a sod of earth in Templeport Lake with a small church and burial ground of twenty-five headstones. It is now officially closed for funerals except for a select few families whose ancestors already have the privilege of being interred there. It is not difficult to see why people should wish to be laid to rest in such a peaceful and beautiful location.

It is said that the soil that clings to the inside walls of the island church has the power to protect the possessor from sudden death, particularly from fire and drowning. So powerful is this Mogue's Clay that it is said to have saved the life of one Mary McGovern of Corlough, who travelled on the ill-fated liner, the *Titanic* and who carried some of the sacred clay on her person.

On a dark and stormy St Patrick's night in 1943, the island was the scene one of the defining incidences of Cavan's history. On that fateful night, a Beaufighter aeroplane JL710 took off from the airstrip at Port Ellen in Scotland on a routine test flight to the Mediterranean region. On board were Pilot Richard Kutura and Navigator Tommy Hulme. During the flight bad weather took its toll, a situation exacerbated by a damaged radio and dwindling fuel.

Hardly being able to see and with warning signals flashing on the dash, the pilot decided that there was no option but to eject. They strapped on their parachutes and when they were over a seemingly sparsely populated area, they left the aircraft.

Shortly afterwards they set down safely in nearby Corlough and Swanlinbar and watched helplessly as their plane carried on unmanned through the night sky. The loud noise of the engine brought people out of their houses from far and wide to watch, with many of the people coming from a dance in the nearby workhouse. They witnessed the plane slowly spiralling downwards until it finally crashed into Templeport Lake at the edge of St Mogue's Island. The pilot and the navigator made their way over the border into the north.

The locals went in search of the aircraft across the lake and bog in an effort to help; some even got lost along the way. Seeing the tail of the aircraft protruding from the lake at the island, a local rector by the name of Armstrong got into his small boat and rowed out to see if there was anybody still onboard, but seeing that there was not, he quickly departed for fear of an explosion.

For weeks afterwards, divers went out to the wreckage, taking souvenirs. It was not long before the army took control of the wreckage and brought the remaining craft over the border to be taken by RAF officials there.

Nobody who was in the area on that night will forget the chaotic excitement that happened when the Beaufighter aircraft crashed on their little island. Some even say that the RAF men have St Mogue to thank for their safe delivery home.

2

LEGENDARY FIGURES

FINN MACCOOL'S FINGERS

Finn MacCool, also known as Fionn MacCumhaill (which is the version I personally prefer) was no ordinary giant. He was a man of epic proportions in every sense of the word.

Of all the men and beasts in the land, he was the biggest and strongest of them all. Said to stand at a whopping 52½ft tall, Finn could lift whole towns in his enormous hands and his voice could be heard from Antrim to Kerry, and as far away as the mighty kingdom of the Isle of Man.

He led an eventful life, full of mischief, bravery, and adventure, from the shaping of Ireland's coastline to the fighting of spirits, from battling other giants to leading the High King's private army as its commander-in-chief.

One day, whilst meeting with his beloved soldiers at their garrison fort, message reached Finn of High King Cairbre's request for the marriage of his daughter to Maolsheachlainn, Prince of the Déisi. Now, Finn, fiercely knowing the difference from right and wrong, knew of Cairbre's hand in the death of Maolsheachlainn's father Oengus, and he was very unhappy with this arrangement.

Finn found himself in a predicament: stand up against the High King, and in the process cause much bloodshed, or allow the marriage go ahead as planned. He discussed the situation with his men and decided that the best compromise, although not ideal, was to seek a hefty payment in lieu of their support for the match. Finn thought that this would make their feelings known whilst at the same time keeping the peace. He was to be severely mistaken.

High King Cairbre was furious at Finn's insolence and decided that such treachery should only be met by force of arms. Raising his army, he ordered them to track down Finn and his men and not to return unless they carried the Fianna's severed heads with them as proof of their defeat.

They marched across the countryside and came to the plain at Gabhra, not far from royal seat of Tara, where they saw the Fianna on parade in strict military alignment.

They heard Finn roaring the Fianna's mottoes:

'Glaine ár gcroí. Neart ár ngéag. Beart de réir ár mbriathar.'
('Purity of our hearts. Strength of our limbs. Action to match our speech.')

Following this, the Fianna sounded the war cry, the famous Dorn Fiann, by blowing their horn – the *borabu* – three times, and charged towards Cairbre's men. When the two armies clashed, there was such ferocity that the ground trembled and sparks flew from their swords. The screams of the fallen could be heard for miles around.

It is said that on that day the plain of Gabhra ran red with blood and the mighty river that once drained the lands of water now drained it of the blood of the fallen warriors.

Finn sank to his knees in tears when he realised that the battle was all but lost. Not only had he lost many good comrades and friends, but he also lost both his son, Oisín, and grandson, Oscar, in the massacre.

When the fighting had subsided and Cairbre's victorious men had left the battlefield, Finn placed a standing stone on the site of the battle and, picking up the horn, gathered his men and retreated in mournful silence some 35 miles over the border until he reached the entrance to the Otherworld in Breffni.

He entered the cave and, laying his fallen men down around him, vowed that when Ireland needs their help, the Dorn Fiann must be sounded three times and he would rise once again with his

restored men to protect the land. He then pushed his hand through the ceiling of the cave and he fell into a deep slumber. Over time the sun had bleached his exposed fingers and turned them to stone. They can be seen to this day on Shantemon Mountain and they are known by all as 'Finn MacCool's Fingers'.

St Patrick and the Idol of Crom Cruach

I have long been fascinated by the Killycluggin stone, which sat between two rivers in the very historic and ancient place within the present-day County Cavan area known as Magh Slecht.

Magh Slecht loosely translates from the old tongue as 'Plain of Prostrations' and is believed to point to the area being a place of worship of the old gods and the old ways.

Although the original stone now sits in pieces in the excellent Cavan County Museum in Ballyjamesduff, there is a replica of how the stone may have looked set at the side of the road near Ballyconnell.

It is believed that this stone represented the pagan Crom Cruach, known as the Irish Sun God and the god of all gods. This fairly unassuming carved stone was covered in precious gold and silver and positioned in pride of place within a circle of twelve idols. It was worshipped by the native Irish.

The legend of Crom Cruach is a dark and sinister one. The ancient texts of the Metrical Dindshenchas claim that the people worshipped the god by offering up their firstborn child in return for a plentiful harvest in the coming year. The children were brutally killed by the established process of smashing their heads against the stone, which represented Crom Cruach, and their blood was sprinkled around the base.

One day on the eve of the new year festival of Samhain (forerunner to the present-day Hallowe'en), the High King Tigernmas

had travelled with his court in procession from his royal seat
at Tara to the idol of Crom Cruach at Magh Slecht in order to
worship him. Whilst they were prostrating in deep devotion to
their deity, their druids were preparing the sacrifices to be put to
death.

St Patrick and his disciples were watching the proceedings from
a nearby hill and just before the forced slaying of the innocent, he
reached out the Bachal Isu, or staff of Christ, which miraculously
reached from the neighbouring hill with such force that the Crom
Cruach stone collapsed, falling forward with its head symbolically
pointing towards Tara.

St Patrick then came down off the hill with his brethren and, taking a sledgehammer, smashed the stone, causing the Devil within to emerge with horrific growls and roars. St Patrick then struck his staff on the remaining rubble of the idol, and banished him to hell. The twelve idols surrounding Crom Cruach were then swallowed up by the earth.

The original Killycluggin stone in Cavan County Museum is in fact the same Crom Cruach, and its shattered appearance is testament to the pivotal role it played in the conversion of the local pagans.

BALOR AND THE *GLAS GAIBHEANN*

Stories from the ancients spread far and wide across the land, and some, like the mighty tale of Balor of the Mighty Blows or Balor of the Evil Eye were truly universal and told around the hearths of many a Cavan family, striking fear into many a *gosoon*.

Many years ago, there lived a young lad, who was, to say the least, a wee bit unusual. You see, Balor did not look like everybody else. Instead of two eyes like the rest of us, he had one big eye set right in the centre of his forehead. If this were not bad enough, he had also been afflicted with the unfortunate condition, which was known as the *Birach-derc* or 'speary eye', whereby whomever he looked at would immediately die.

Balor lived on Tory Island with his people, the Formorians, and the Formorians were a little more preoccupied than most with making warfare against their enemies, the Tuath Dé Danann.

Now, when he was not much more than a whippet, he passed by a grove where a druidical ritual was taking place. The druids were preparing spells of death that they could take into war with the Tuath Dé Danann. Even though he knew he should not, Balor watched the druids stirring the cauldron, when a spark shot out and hit him in the eye.

He cried out in agony and the druids came to see what the commotion was. On realising what had happened, they knew that the spell of death had gone into Balor's eye and that anyone he looked at with that eye from that day on would die. To protect his own people, he had to keep his eye closed among them but whenever he went into battle all he had to do was open his eye and his enemies would immediately fall down dead before him.

Balor grew up to be king of the Formorians and a fierce and fearless pirate. Knowing of the prophesy that he would be killed by his own grandchild, he imprisoned his daughter Eithne in a tower of glass, guarded by twelve women, who were forbidden to disclose the existence of men to her.

Feeling confident that there was no way he could be killed, he became reckless and vicious in his raiding up and down the land. He had set his eye on a magical cow, called the Glas Gaibheann, known never to cease giving milk. This cow was owned by Cian, the king of the Tuath Dé Danann, his sworn enemies.

One day, Cian and his brother Samthain went to meet the smith to have new swords forged. Cian left Samthain holding the magical cow's leash and went inside to make the arrangements. Balor, spotting his chance, used magic to disguise himself as a redheaded child and told Samthain that he overheard Cian say that he would have a magnificent sword made and that there would be no more steel left for Samthain. Falling hook, line, and sinker for this lie, Samthain became enraged and, leaving the cow outside, stormed into the forge looking for an explanation. Cian knew that something rotten was afoot and rushed outside, but it was too late; both Balor and the Glas Gaibheann were gone.

Cian was determined to get his cow back, so he visited a druidess called Birog of the Mountain. Birog knew that Cian would not get

his cow back whilst Balor was alive because of his evil eye but she was also aware of the prophesy of Balor's death, so they hatched a plan between them. Cian disguised himself as a woman and Birog conjured up a wind and blew them both across the sea to the glass tower where Eithne was imprisoned.

Cian, still disguised as a woman, said that he was Queen of the Tuath Dé Danann and was being chased by her enemies and needed shelter. Eithne instructed her women to open up the doors, and he ascended the tower to her. They fell in love at first sight, and, realising that Cian was not all he initially appeared to be, they made love there and then.

Eithne soon found out that she was carrying a child, and in time gave birth to a son, who she named Lugh – Balor's grandchild. Knowing that this child was prophesised to end his life, Balor seized him and threw him into the sea. Birog of the Mountain was watching and saved the baby in time, returning him to his father.

In many years, Lugh grew to be a fine man and a fine warrior. In time, he fulfilled the prophecy and put his own grandfather to death on the battlefield at Moytura.

AN GOBÁN SAOR

An Gobán Saor, or Gobán the Builder, was a carpenter, mason, architect, and general first-rate tradesman at all things. It is believed that, although he travelled the world, he spent most of his days in the present-day area of Tullygobban in the Cavan Burren, where his wife and son are said to be buried to this day.

He was highly sought after by kings, princes, and the wealthy alike, and his skill of working with wood and stone preceded him. Many of the wondrous churches, palaces, fortresses, and tombs that exist to this day all across the world can be attributed to this master.

As it was in those days, the blessing of the master was required for any bethrothal in the household. Being a very smart man, the Gobán decided to give his son a challenge to see if he was really prepared to take a wife and so he gave him a sheepskin and said, '*Ara gosoon*, you'll have my blessing only when you bring this skin back to me with also the price of it. Until you do, you'll not be getting my blessing to marry.' The son carried the sheepskin under his arm to Arvagh every month, but he could never find anybody to give him the skin and also the price of it.

There was a fine girl who saw the young lad at the market every month and was very perplexed at what he was up to month in, month out, so she asked him what his game was. He explained the situation of it to her, so she took the sheepskin off him, plucked the wool off it and went into the merchant shop. She came out just a few minutes later after selling the wool, giving him back the skin and the money for it. The Gobán was so impressed with this that he gave his blessing for the marriage between them to go ahead.

SETANTA AND THE HOUND OF CULAINN

Setanta was a fine strappin' lad who was gifted with superhuman strength, speed and skill. Born of Dechtire, his mother, and the God Lugh, he always wanted to put his immense skills to good use by joining the Red Branch knights.

Unfortunately, his mother would not allow him to go off to join the Red Branch as he was too young so he sent him off to his uncle, Conor MacNessa, who was King of Ulster, and ultimately of East Bréifne, or present-day Cavan.

When Setanta was seven years old, he and his uncle were invited to a meal at the fort of his spear maker, a man by the name of Culainn.

Setanta was busy chopping wood, and so told the king to go on ahead of him and that he would follow when he finished his work. Culainn thought that the king was the last guest to arrive and so he unchained his massive wolfhound to keep guard around the perimeter of the fort.

When Setanta had finished chopping and stacking the wood, he followed his uncle to the fort of Culainn but when he arrived, he heard the sound of growling. Not knowing what he was about to encounter, he slowly began to retreat but then he saw the largest wolfhound he had ever seen. It had red, glowing eyes, and white froth poured from its gigantic fangs. The wolfhound circled Setanta a few times and then stopped for a moment before pouncing at him from a standing start. Without thinking, Setanta quickly drew his hurley and, with a slight of his hand, hurled the sliotar down the throat of the animal, killing it instantly.

All within the fort heard the commotion outside and ran out to see what was happening. King Conor had realised what had happened and was extremely impressed with his nephew's strength and skill. Setanta said to Culainn, 'Allow me to take the place of your hound until you find another', to which Culainn duly agreed.

From that day forward, Setanta became known as Cúchulainn or 'the Hound of Culainn'.

CORMAC MÓR AND CORMAC BEAG

Long ago before the advent of Christianity, there lived in the townland of Aghalattafraal a chieftain by the name of Cormac Mór of the O'Farrell sept. He was a great landowner, had many cows and – seeing as cows were currency back in that time – he was very wealthy. His small family consisted of himself, his beautiful wife, and one fine son named Cormac Beag.

Cormac Beag had great potential, but was too easy-going for his own good and did not reach the standard of cleverness that his parents had hoped and wished for. In fact, his lack of intelligence gave rise to a great deal of anxiety for his parents, and their druid suggested that they take him on a visit to a friend by the Lough of Andoul, a place at the extreme end of the kingdom, as this visit might improve his education.

As they were walking along the lakeshore at Andoul, they saw a strange man row in and land his boat on the shingle. Neither Cormac Mór nor Cormac Beag recognised this man. He spoke to Cormac Mór and asked him if the boy with him was his son, to which he replied that he was, but that both he and his wife were greatly disappointed with the stupidity of the young lad. The man said that if they would give him the child, he would keep him for a whole year and return him after this time as one of the cleverest men in the whole kingdom.

When Cormac Mór told his wife this, she was in deep distress at the thought of parting with her only child, but she had only to wait patiently for the year to elapse. So they both agreed and the boy was taken away by the boatman to achieve a fine mind. At the end of the prescribed time Cormac Mór kissed his wife goodbye and said he would be back the following day with their son. He again visited Andoul and on reaching the small lough excitedly saw the man rowing in with Cormac Beag rowing beside him.

When the boat came close to the shore, Cormac Mór thought it strange that his son did not speak. The man said, 'Sure enough I told you I would bring your son back in one year, and I have kept that promise. I did not, however, promise to give him to you!' and with that, he turned the boat around and went back out onto the lough. Poor Cormac Mór was grieved beyond consolation and knew that he would not be able to go home to his wife without their son.

Cormac Mór frantically ran along the coast and, seeing a small boat nearby, quickly boarded it and went in pursuit of Cormac Beag and his kidnapper. After a time he reached the other side of the lough and abandoned the boat. He saw Cormac Beag running towards him with the man running behind. 'The man is a magician and has a spell over me to keep me here,' said the son. 'Listen to me and I will tell you how to rescue me.' He told his father where the man's ash wand was kept and explained that if he snapped it in two, then all the spells would be broken, including the one to make him smart.

Cormac Mór pretended to go away but instead went to the place under a stone where the wand could be found. He split it over his knee and his fine son was free once more, although all the less clever. 'I am so sorry, my Cormac Beag, for making you come here,' said he.

DIARMUID AND GRÁINNE

Many stories are told across the land of the plight of Diarmuid and Gráinne, and here and there throughout the country are places said to have various connections with them.

There is one such place in the townland of Achawee, or 'yellow field', in the barony of Clanmahon, not far from the village of Kilnaleck. It is at this place that Diarmuid and Gráinne are said to have slept whilst fleeing the jealous pursuit of the mighty Fionn MacCumhaill.

I should bring the story back a little bit and explain that Gráinne, who was the most beautiful woman in Ireland, but also the daughter of Cormac Mac Airt, the High King of all Ireland, was pursued for romance by many of Ireland's rich, famous, and most eligible of males – chieftains, princes, and kings alike. The mighty Fionn MacCumhaill even set his sights on the beauty and asked that she allow him to take her hand as his second wife.

The young lady accepted Fionn's proposal and the Fianna threw a grand banquet for them to celebrate the fantastic news of their leader and his new woman. On the very same evening of the celebration, whilst Fionn was dozing from too much food and too much mead, Gráinne became acquainted with one of his best generals, a fine strapping lad by the name of Diarmuid. Diarmuid was young and strong, unlike the ageing Fionn. Her heart began to thump uncontrollably, so much so that she thought it would jump right out of her chest! Little did she know at that time that Diarmuid was also experiencing the same sensation. They both knew at that very moment that they had fallen utterly and deeply in love, a love so strong and so rare that nothing could part them from that point forward.

Gráinne was prepared to do whatever was necessary to make Diarmuid hers and so she prepared a potion and slipped it into the big bowl of mead that sat at the end of the grand table in the banquet hall. It had the effect of making Fionn's men fall into a deep, but temporary, slumber.

Knowing that they did not have much time, the two lovers then made their escape and set out over the land to make a new life together. Just as they left the hall, Fionn awoke and saw the couple depart and, realising what was happening, he flew into a blind fit of rage. He let out a loud roar, stood up and turned over the table in anger, sending all the food and drink crashing everywhere. He roused the men and ordered them to prepare for the pursuit of the two traitors.

The two eloped and were chased all across the land, hiding and sleeping in all manner of nooks, crannies and caves. They were pursued by a furious Fionn, with his soothsayer and army of men. Diarmuid was very smart, and wherever they slept, he played a trick so as to confuse the soothsayer. If they slept on the beach,

he would gather up heather from the mountains and they would make a bed from it, and if they slept in the mountains he would gather up sand from the beach and again make a bed from it. The soothsayer would tell Fionn what the couple slept on and so send them off track.

After many years on the run, Gráinne became pregnant with Diarmuid's child, but fate was about to turn for the worse and one day whilst out in the wilderness, a giant boar confronted them. This was very bad news for Diarmuid, for legend had foretold that the only living creature that could harm him was a wild boar. The boar snorted and stamped his hooves on the ground and suddenly charged at the couple. Diarmuid stepped out in front of his lady to protect her from the beast and was gored by one of his tusks. He yelped out in pain and drew his sword, slicing the animal's head from its body. He fell to the ground with the life being sucked from him. Gráinne cradled her love's head in her arms and wept.

With that, Fionn and his men came upon the couple and Gráinne begged him to cure Diarmuid with a drink of magic water from his cupped hands. Fionn laughed heavily and spat on the ground. 'I'll not be saving any traitor on this day!' His soldiers also begged Fionn to do something as they knew that Diarmuid was a good man with a noble heart. Finally, Fionn's son, Oisín pulled his sword out and said, 'If you will not save Diarmuid from death, then it will be you that will join him on this day!'

Fionn agreed to help but by then it was too late and Diarmuid had died in the arms of his lover.

BRICÍN THE SURGEON

Many people will be forgiven for thinking that brain surgery is a modern invention; I know I certainly did. There is no doubt that it will surprise a lot of people to learn that well over 1,000 years ago such procedures were being carried out in the present-day border parish of Tomregan, between the counties of Cavan and Fermanagh.

Located in the ancient kingdom of Bréifne, the area of Tuaim Dreacuin was a famous district of learning, having, as it did, an ancient university that contained three colleges within: one for Brehon Law, one for History and Poetry, and one for Classical Learning. Among its celebrated staff was a professor known as Bricín, a highly respected saint, a distinguished scholar, and an outstanding surgeon. His fame spread far and wide, and many came seeking advice and assistance for the various ailments they suffered from.

One day, Bricín was teaching in class when there was a great commotion outside. A carriage came thundering through the gateway and he could hear the panicked shouts of men saying, '*Cá bhfuil Bricín?* Where is Bricín?'

He came rushing out, asking, '*Cad é an fadhb?* What is the problem?'

Barely able to talk from exhaustion, the men were just able to utter, 'Battle … Uloira … hopelessly outnumbered …'. Bricín walked around and, looking into the carriage, immediately recognised Cennfaelad, one of the chieftains of Ulster. Cennfaelad was in a bad way, with a large axe protruding from the top of his head and blood streaming from the wound and running down his face. The prognosis was not a good one at all.

Bricín called to two of his students. 'Prepare the operating room,' said he, and to another two, he said, 'Take the chieftain and prepare him for surgery.' Bricín then went and washed his hands in the stream and collected some healing herbs that he needed for the operation.

Telling the soldiers that he must not be disturbed, he worked long and hard on Cennfaelad. First, he controlled the bleeding and then slowly and carefully removed the axe from his skull. It was only at this point that he was fully able to see the full extent of the damage. Bricín set about removing the damaged tissue with

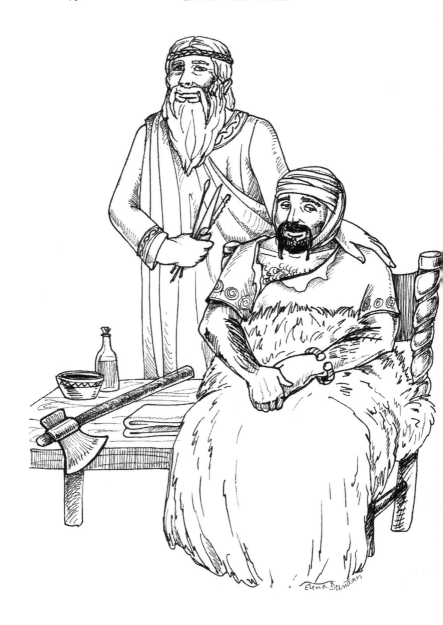

his specialised scalpel and repairing what remained with his other tools.

After two days straight, the surgery was completed. Bricín placed a thick layer of healing herbs over the wound and bandaged up Cennfaelad's head. He gave strict orders for the chieftain's undisturbed rest and convalescence at the university. During this time, Bricín tended to him day and night, and slowly Cennfaelad regained his strength and came out of his coma.

Save for a slight twitch in his left eye, Cennfaelad had fully recovered. His memory was completely restored and he was infinitely grateful for what Bricín had done for him. He developed a keen interest in studying at the three colleges of the university, and following through on this, went on to become one of its most distinguished scholars and poets. Cennfaelad produced three famous works, on law, Irish grammar and contemporary history.

3

FABLED PLACES

MAGUIRE'S CHAIR

Maguire's Chair is the name given to a great rock on the side of the road at Blackrock's Cross in Altachullion. It is said that this fine carved seat is the inauguration site and place of convention of the chief of the mighty Maguire clan. So revered was this place that, not only was the Maguire crowned at this place; he also witnessed agreements, settled disputes, and passed judgments on persons deemed to have done wrong.

Wisdom of the Chieftain
The Maguire was so respected by all that many went to him for advice.

On one such occasion, two particular clans – the O'Rourkes of Leitrim and the McGoverns of Cavan – had come to loggerheads over where each other's territory began and ended. The situation had deteriorated over time to such an extent that a battle was becoming more and more likely between them, as was only too common an occurrence back in the day. On hearing of this situation, the Maguire was greatly concerned and invited both clan leaders to a court at his place of convention.

On arriving at Maguire's Chair, both the McGovern and the O'Rourke sat in nervous suspicion of the other. The Maguire sat and listened to each of the chieftains' grievances and, on hearing the full story, unrolled a large vellum map of the areas in question drawn up by his scribe.

He went through the territories in question in great detail and divided the lands with agreement, ensuring that each clan had the same amount of quality grazing and arable land, and also ensuring that the sites sacred to each remained within their own areas.

They were both so impressed with the negotiations and outcome that they immediately consented to the realignment of the borders, and to the future friendship of their two clans.

The Priest Catcher

During the dark days of the Penal Times, Maguire's Chair was used as a lookout post for priests saying Mass or carrying out their ministries during the time when strict laws imposed by a heartless foreign government prohibited the Irish from practising their religion.

When the British soldiers were in Ireland, nearly everyone had a secret hiding place in the house. There was a small dwelling near this place called Tí Fiac O'Dolan. One night, Fiac's aged mother was very sick and it was unlikely that she would make it through the night. She asked Fiac to fetch the priest, as she would require the last rites.

Fiac did as he was bid and returned with the priest; however, whilst the last sacrament was being administered, Fiac heard the signal from the local *gosoon* keeping watch at Maguire's Chair.

Unfortunately for Fiac, the *gosoon* had fallen asleep at the chair and gave the signal a little too late, by which time the British soldiers were already approaching the house and shouting for the priest to come out immediately. Fiac told the priest to continue with his work, and when the soldiers pounded on the door with the butts of their guns, Fiac threw on an aul black shawl belonging to his mother, opened the door and told them that he was the priest. The soldiers, believing that they had done their duty, looked no further, took Fiac out by force and hung him from the nearest tree.

The real priest then had to give the last rites to the two O'Dolans.

The Wishing Chair

Whilst so much violence surrounds the history of our beautiful county, not everything was so sad. Maguire's Chair was the location of many a happy childhood scene for so many.

It was a very popular place for dancing, games, and bilberry picking, particularly on the last Sunday of July, which was known as Garlic, Donagh, or Bilberry Sunday.

It was customary to sit on the chair on this day and make a personal wish; if done so with a good heart, it would come true.

Many a happy marriage has also come from happy times at Maguire's Chair.

MOGUE OF INIS BRÉACHMHAIGH

On the lough of Templeport lies a small unassuming island, but with an impressive history. Formerly known as Inis Bréachmhaigh, meaning 'island of the plain of wolves', these days this sodden clump of earth is better known under several names – those of Port, Inch, or St Mogue's Island. However, none sound as dramatic as the former. It was on this island that St Mogue, otherwise known as St Aiden, the famous bishop of Ferns, was born.

Mogue had gold plated ancestry on both sides of his family, God be good to him, with both his mammy and his daddy being of royal lineage.

One night, long before Mogue was born, his parents were asleep when a bright star descended from the heavens and rested on each of them. All around had seen this impressive sight and knew that this was a sure sign of the future greatness of their unborn son.

Even before he was born, Mogue was to be known as 'Son of the Star' for the entirety of his life. Many believed that there were striking similarities between the Star of Bethlehem and this occurrence, and knew that he was to be very holy indeed.

St Killan of Fenagh woke one morning and saw that there was a heavy snowfall overnight. Now in itself, there is nothing unusual about a bit of a flurry, except for the fact that it was smack bang in the middle of an unusually hot summer. He went out to herd his cattle into the byre to protect them against the inclement weather, and saw that they were down on the shore of the lake gazing in awe towards the island. Knowing that this meant the child was born, he prepared himself for a baptism.

The woman who lived on the island was frantic to help the child get over to be baptised, but as her husband was out on the lake, she had no boat. She placed the child on the enormous flag hearth in her cottage when suddenly it moved with a sudden jerk. The hearthstone then gently and smoothly slid out the door and down to the shore. When, to her amazement it took to the water and miraculously started to float over to the mainland to St Killan, who was waiting.

When the baptism was complete, the young Mogue was returned to his parents on the island by the same miraculous means, along with the gift of a bell.

For many years afterwards, the stone continued to provide safe passage to those visiting the church on the island, until one day a young couple jumped on the stone to test its powers. It departed from the mainland and floated out onto the water as it had done on many occasions before, but this time was different, as the stone was greatly offended. Halfway over to the island, the stone cracked in the middle and half sank to the bottom, taking the couple with it, whereas the remaining half continued on its journey and came to rest on the shoreline of the island, where it remains to this day.

THE RED ROAD TO ARVA

The road into Arva in the county of Cavan originates in the neighbouring county of Leitrim and it is known by all around as 'The Red Road to Arva'. The story behind why the road has been given this name goes back to the time of our patron saint.

St Patrick was travelling along this way when hunger came upon him. He noticed a house on the road and hoped to call in there and seek some nourishment. He knocked on the door and the woman who answered put her foot in his way so that he could not enter. Eventually he persuaded her to let him in and as he sat down, he asked if he could have some food to allow him continue on his way. The woman, being very stingy, would not give him any good meat so she went out the back and killed the cat and had it served up for him on a plate. Before commencing the meal, St Patrick made the sign of the cross and touched the cat and it immediately jumped off the table and went in the direction of Arva. All along behind it was a trail of blood, and it is from this reason that the road forever became known as 'The Red Road to Arva'.

The Worm Ditch

Claí na Péiste is known by various names in various places across the land of Ireland. Names such as the Black Pig's Dyke or Race, the Rut, the Valley, or – in our own fair county and neighbouring Monaghan – the Worm Ditch, are all attributed to a massive and strange earthwork that runs across the countryside.

In the county of Cavan, the story here goes thus:

Long ago in Ireland, there lived many races of fantastical creatures of all shapes and sizes. Now, some of these creatures lived in peace with each other and with their neighbours, and others did not.

There was once a hedge school down by the townland of Ardkill, and this hedge school was run by a secretive but brilliant master. Little did the local people know that the master was a powerful magician, who practised incantations on their children for his own amusement.

Paddy's son came home every day with a ferocious appetite on him; so hungry was he that Paddy could hardly keep him full, and he also had a large brood to feed. 'It's only school you've been to on this day. You'll be getting the same lot of food that the rest of the clan get.'

The *gosoon* then told his father, 'The master turns me into a hare during the school, and the others into hounds, and they run after me for the chase. This is the reason behind my ravishment.' Paddy became furious but, holding himself back, said he'd go down the following day and have a word with this master. The next day came, and Paddy went down and asked the master, 'Is it true that you turn the children into beasts?'

'It is, Sir,' said the master.

'Can you show me and turn yourself into a goat?'

'I can, Sir,' said the master, and with that, he opened his spell book, recited the incantation and transformed himself into a goat. He then tapped his foot on the floor and changed back into human form.

'Can you turn yourself into a pig?'

'I can, Sir,' said the master, and with that, turned over another page in his book, recited the incantation and transformed himself into a pig. He then tapped his foot on the floor and changed back into human form.

With this, the father then said, 'Can you turn yourself into a *péist*?'

'I can, Sir,' said the master, 'but I will need a little more room for that.'

They went outside and sat down on the grass. The master turned over a page in his book, recited the incantation, as before, and transformed himself into an immense and horrific worm. Grabbing the spell book, Paddy ran into the school and threw it on to the fire. Seeing what Paddy did, the master tried to tap his foot on the ground, but he could not as he was a *péist*, with no arms and no legs.

The book burned quickly and the master let out a loud screech, all the while writhing in agony. He made for the coast in the hope of relief and wrecked his way through the land all along the way, tunnelling through the earth and forcing it up into long ramparts in the process.

He finally got to the sea, but little relief was there as the tide took him out and he drowned.

THE GIANT'S LEAP

With a limestone landscape similar to that of the Burren in County Clare, the natural landscape of the Cavan Burren was hugely altered with the plantation of many trees in the 1950s, giving it a much different look than would otherwise have been the case.

Many years ago, there were two brothers named Brendan and Fiachra. Nothing unusual there, you might think, but Brendan and Fiachra were not usual; they were members of the giant people.

Some stories may have you thinking that giants were only interested in fighting and hurting each other, but this could not be further from the truth in this case. Not only were the brothers family – they were also best friends. Brendan and Fiachra lived in the same house, went out hunting together, ate together and played cards together of an evening. Giants were not a common sight in the area, so they made sure to mind each other.

One day, Brendan went out for a walk on his own and sat down by the river whilst whistling a sweet tune to himself. 'That's a lovely tune,' said a voice from further along the riverbank. Brendan looked around and saw the most beautiful woman he had ever seen and she was a giant too. 'What are the odds?' he thought to himself.

'My name is Sorcha,' said the young lass. Brendan and Sorcha spent the rest of the day together, until it began to get dark and they both parted ways. However, they agreed to see each other again soon.

Brendan rushed home to tell Fiachra that he had fallen in love, but when he got home, Fiachra was already asleep, and he remembered that he would arise early the next day for to move the sheep to the higher fields.

Fiachra was up and gone the next morning before Brendan even stirred in his bed. He took his crook and headed for the lower field. Along the bottom of this field ran the river and Fiachra could hear the sound of a woman singing, so he went to investigate.

He looked around and saw the most beautiful woman he had ever seen, and she was a giant too. 'What are the odds?' he thought to himself.

'My name is Sorcha,' said the young lass. Fiachra forgot about the sheep and spent hours with Sorcha. 'I've fallen in love', thought he to himself.

Brendan awoke some time later and went looking for Fiachra to tell him of his great news, when he spotted Fiachra with Sorcha down by the river. They seemed a little more than comfortable in each other's company.

Brendan challenged Fiachra and Sorcha, and a fistfight nearly broke out. They agreed to have a competition, and whoever won would win Sorcha's hand.

Sorcha set them the challenge that whoever jumped quickest across over the chasm and back three times would win her hand. The two brothers set themselves up, and Sorcha sat on a large rock nearby to watch the competition.

Fiachra went first and, taking a running jump, made it across to the other side of the chasm with great ease. He did the same on the way back over with a little more difficulty, and on the third occasion he jumped and climbed up from the edge, as the tiredness took its toll.

Brendan then took his turn, and like his brother, took a run and jump over to the other side and back again. Visibly out of breath, he ran and jumped the third time but he only reached the very edge. He grasped the clumps of grass and began to climb up, but they came loose. To both Fiachra's and Sorcha's horror, they saw him slip and fall to his death. In great distress, Fiachra and Sorcha went to the bottom of the chasm and buried poor Brendan's body under a large stone grave.

To this day, the area is known as the Giant's Leap.

How Lough Gowna was Formed

One day a woman went down to a holy well to wash clothes; the type of thing that someone just should not do.

When she was finished washing the dirty socks, out jumped a calf from the well. She got such a shock that she ran away, but the calf ran after her and the well began to overflow. The silly woman fell three times, and each time she did the water went around that spot, creating islands in the newly formed lough. She eventually keeled over and died from exhaustion.

The Irish name for the lake is Loch Gomhna meaning 'Lake of the Calf'.

The Nine Yew Trees of Derrylane

Overlooking the very scenic loughs of Derrylane and Derrybrick is a beautiful and remote place, which houses a fine old abbey ruin and round tower. It is said that it was established by St Colmcille and run by St Mogue. Although this place is very ancient, it is still used as a burial place to this day for many of the families in the parish. At one time in the area surrounding the sacred ground grew nine yew trees, of which eight were said to have sprung up in one single night.

There was once a local lad who had a yearning to serve God and who knew that his calling was to be a priest. This lad also had a female friend, who also knew that she had a vocation to serve God, and to become a nun. This pair had a very soft spot for each other but knew that once they embarked on their individual religious journeys that they could no longer see each other as this would contravene the vows that they were about to take. This greatly saddened them, so much so that they questioned the decisions they were making. 'Why can't we marry and also serve God?' they thought.

Alas, they could not do both, and so they took the bold and brave decision to elope. They packed up their meagre belongings and, telling nobody, agreed to meet at the grand big yew tree that grew near the old ruins.

He arrived first and waited at the yew, becoming impatient when she did not show. He saw a second yew in the distance that he had not noticed growing there before and thought that his beloved was probably waiting there, so he headed through the rushy field to it, but on arriving there saw that she was not there either. Again, he saw yet another yew tree in the distance and again, thinking she could be there, he went further on. At the end of it all, he visited nine yew trees – although he could only ever remember one growing there ever before. He came to the sad conclusion that he was being stood up and went off on his own to enrol in the monastery.

In a bizarre twist of fate, she was also going from yew to yew searching for her beloved, before she came to the conclusion that he was not coming, and she also left for the nunnery. The next day, the people could not believe that there were nine ancient yew trees growing where there was only one the previous night.

It is said that God placed the yew trees there in one night so as to ensure the couple continued on the path that he had set out for them.

4

ANCIENT KNOWLEDGE

CURES

The witches of *Macbeth*, stirring their large cauldron and chanting their spells '*Eye of newt and toe of frog …* ' could well have been related to some of our own ancient and modern healers of the land. Healing mumps, sties, warts, headaches, and even worms, many of our superstitions and remedies do appear to be strange on the face of them – but who are we to balk at an ancient skill that has clearly worked for many just because we don't understand it?

Herbal medicine in Ireland is a thread that refuses to be broken, and is actually currently seeing a resurgence in interest, with new knowledge, learning and research showing that it is not all nonsense, like so many would have us believe. Many of the myriad illnesses to which the human being may succumb respond to the healing powers of the plants that grow in the fields, bogs, and meadows.

This botanical and sometimes faith-based medicine is the traditional and indigenous medicine of the Irish. It is a knotted, tangled, almost broken – but not quite – thread of a system that cared well for Irish society until its displacement and dislodgement in the political turmoil of our history.

I have included here a number of cures that were, and continue to be, used by the many Cavan locals over the millennia.

Mumps

A person whose mother's surname has not been changed by marriage is supposed to have a cure for mumps. The person suffering from mumps has a halter put on them and is led to a stream by the curer. The curer then takes three drops of water, one after another, in his hand in honour of the Blessed Trinity and gives them to the person to drink. This is done for three days in succession and the mumps will be cured after this period.

Stye in the Eye

To cure a style in the eye, collect ten gooseberry thorns, throw one away and point the remaining nine at the stye and then order the stye away in Irish. It will disappear if this is done for nine successive days.

Dead Hand

The hand of a corpse was believed to be a cure for all diseases. Sick people would be brought to a house where a corpse was laid out so that the hand could be laid on them.

Warts

A wart is a little lump of flesh that grows on the hands. If you meet a black slug when not expecting it, pick it up and rub him on your wart. Then stick him on a thorn of a *sceach* (poor little *craythur*). This treatment must be repeated twice a week, on a Tuesday and Thursday, using the same snail, and when he withers away, so will the wart.

Worms

The following method was used to test whether a child had worms or not. A folded tape was placed under the arm of the suspected victim and the arm was squeezed lightly on it to hold it in position. Whilst the tape was under the arm, the person who had the cure knelt down and said certain prayers. The tape was then examined and if it remained rolled up tightly, the suspected victim was free from worms but if the tape was loose, it indicated that the child was infected. If the presence of worms was discovered, the following cure was administered: come coprice was dissolved in water and this was drunk on nine successive mornings. It was only certain families who possessed this cure. It was hereditary and was usually practised by one member of the family only, although every member had the cure.

Burns

Candles used at funerals were thought to have curative powers. The butts of the candles would be saved to cure burns by rubbing them on the affected area and saying particular prayers for the persons recovery.

Corns

Corns are a prevalent skin disease. They grow mostly on the toes and are very painful, especially (as the old people say) when the rain is coming. Bog water is a good cure for them, and the affected foot has to be saturated in a pool of bog water for some time. When the foot is taken out the corn is picked off.

Water Retention

Nettles gathered from a churchyard and boiled down into a drink were believed to cure water retention.

Measles

The person who has the measles feels very warm with the disease lasting nine days. During the first three days, the red spots appear and stay out for a further three days. They then take three days to go away. If you mix boiled nettle roots with ass's milk and drink the lot, it will cure the disease.

Stomach Pain

The cure for a pain in the stomach is to get water grass (which is what many of the Irish call watercress) in the morning when you are fasting and eat it.

Heartburn

The cure for heartburn is to get briar leaves and chew them. Another cure is to eat the tops of briars.

Whooping Cough

Milk an ass that is rearing a foal. The person who is suffering is to drink the milk and this will cure them.

Anxiety

Our ancestors believed that the clippings of the hair and nails of a child tied in linen and placed under the ill person's bed would cure convulsions and fretting.

Sore Throat

The cure for a sore throat is to get a rag and fill it with salt that has been roasted on the fire. Put the still-warm salt on your neck and this will cure it.

Canker Sores

Canker sores are lumps that grow around the mouth. The cure for it is to go to the forge and wash your mouth in the water that the blacksmith cools his irons in. This must be done before the sun rises.

Headache

The cure for a headache is to put vinegar on brown paper and put it to your forehead and you will be cured.

The corner of the sheet used to wrap a corpse was also used to cure a headache or a swollen limb.

Another cure for headache is the placing of a cloth on the forehead that has been left out on St Brigid's Eve to receive her blessing as she passes over the land.

Elf-shot

Cattle are sometimes supposed to be 'elf shot', an affliction caused by the arrows of the unseen. They suffer from localised swollen limbs and refuse to eat anything; if not treated, they finally die.

The cure is made with a long briar that has rooted itself twice. The briar is measured three times round the body of the animal. During the measuring, a particular rhyme – known only to the curer – is said. This is done each day until the measurement gets smaller and stops when the animal reaches its normal size. This cure is not handed down from one person to another. Anyone who knows the rhyme and gets the proper briar can make this cure.

Hacks

Hacks are little breaks in the flesh on the hands. The cure for them is to go to the forge and wash your hands in the forge water for ten mornings in succession and the hacks will go away.

WEATHER LORE

Over the millennia, the Irish have devised a marvellous array of methods to predict the weather based on natural arrangements.

In the olden times before scientific appliances were invented, people predicted future weather conditions by the appearance of the heavens above them. People knew that the appearance of the sky, the direction of the wind, the behaviour of animals, birds, and insects, and natural features can all reflect changes in weather conditions.

Speaking about and dwelling on the weather, for better or worse, has always been a favourite pastime (some say obsession!) for many an Irish person, rarely being satisfied, as they are, with how it is outside at any given time.

Here are but a few forecasting traditions …

Those faced with a red sunset in summer know that this is a sign of fine, warm weather to come, whilst in winter it is regarded as a sure sign of frost.

A bright ring around the moon is looked upon as a sign of rain, whilst a clear sky and many twinkling stars foretell frost.

Those waking in the morning to a bright rainbow outside look upon this with great alarm as it is a sign of continuous rain; however, a rainbow in the evening is seen as a good sign as it suggests the spell of bad weather is not set to continue.

The wind blowing from the east and south-east is a sign of good weather. A northerly wind is a sign of cold weather, sometimes bringing frost and snow.

When the seagulls come inland, it is a sign of storm. If the swallows fly high it is a sign of fine weather, but if they fly low, it is looked upon as a sure indication of rain. The robin is considered the best weather prophet of all; he becomes so bold as to come into the house looking for something to eat at the approach of snow.

Sheep are also good weather prophets, as they will move into the highlands at the approach of snow. They are afraid that if they remain on low ground the snow from the highlands may slip and cover them.

The donkey usually turns his back to the wind at the approach of rain.

If the dust flies along the road, it is a sign of rain.

The smoke from the farmhouse chimney ascending perpendicularly into the air is a sure sign of fine weather.

However, despite all of the above different methods of foretelling the weather, we are still known as being notoriously bad at predicting the climate.

MOLL'S SHEBEEN

About a hundred years ago an old woman called Moll Traynor lived near Shercock. This old woman had one fine son whose name was Issy and they lived together in a small mud cabin by the old fort at Lisnageer. It was in this little cabin that she kept a *shebeen*, or illicit bar, and she used to make and sell a large quantity of poteen there – without licence – from the spuds Issy grew out back for her.

She was very good at making the poteen and all that bought it sung her praises over its purity and fine taste, but Moll was fierce afraid to sell it because of the police, and she knew only too well that they were stationed in the town and keeping an eye out for this very thing. She kept her still inside the overgrown fort as she knew that nobody ever went in there for fear of upsetting the wee people. She, herself, had little time for superstitions.

From time to time, Issy would take a reel of timber to the town to sell and the old woman would hide the poteen among the sticks so the people would not see it. When Issy had poteen with him, he would wear a collar, and the people knew that this was the sign. Issy would take it to a side road into a back laneway, and the people following him could then buy it from him. It was in this way that both Issy and Moll made their living.

Poor aul Moll came to a sad ending, though. One day, the neighbours saw a plume of black smoke rising from the old fort; on rushing to the place, they found her burned to a cinder beside her poteen still. The locals say to this day that had Moll offered the wee people some of her produce, she may not have ended up the way she did.

Poor Issy never got over the passing of his mammy and was so heartbroken at her loss that he left for Australia not long after, and their little cabin fell down from neglect.

A modern bungalow now stands where Moll once reigned, queen of her *shebeen*.

ANCIENT CRAFTS

Many years ago people had neither the money nor the convenience to visit DIY or hardware shops, or indeed shopping centres. Anything they needed to make their living was made with their own hands, using crafts that were developed over millennia from the ancient skills of our ancestors and handed down through generations.

With the advent of consumerism, sadly many of these crafts have died out, but, thankfully, some have survived. Some are even seeing a revival, which can only been seen as a good thing.

I have listed here some of the skills and crafts of our ancestors. Perhaps readers may even be tempted to try their hand at one?

Candle Making
The people long ago made their own candles, as there were no candles to be had in the few shops that existed then. These candles were made from grease and rushes, with the fat (tallow) coming

from a sheep they had killed. The rushes came from bogs or other such waterlogged areas.

Lime Burning

Lime is burned in great stone kilns, which are built with much care and attention, as no heat must escape when they are fired.

If they are made about the surface of the earth, the walls must be carefully closed with clay, because the kiln must be airtight. They are circular in shape and then walls are carefully built with brick or stone and mortar. A small hole, known as the *púirtín* is made at the bottom of the kiln and a layer of limestone is put on top of it. Alternate layers of turf and limestone are put into the kiln until it is filled. Then the kiln is set on fire by lighting the turn at the *púveín* (kiln) and allowed to burn for three or four days. It is then covered to prevent the rain from getting in at the lime, because it would slake it. The lime is taken out through the *púveín* after some time.

Weaving

In times long gone, people grew their own flax and steeped it in a bog hole. When it was ready, they brought it to the weavers to have it spun into linen.

Basket Making

Long ago, when anything needed carrying, such as turf, a basket or *ciseán* was used. Sally rods that were not very thick were cut and tied in bundles, and the basket maker stuck two rods in the ground in a cruciform shape so that they arched upwards. He would then weave the other rods in and around them in a very specific way until all the rods were able to support themselves without being planted.

Ink Making

All the old people long ago made their own ink. They gathered elderberries and boiled them. When they had them boiled well, they strained the resulting liquid and put more elderberries down to boil in the same water. When they had it well boiled and strained, they put it in bottles. Then they had their own ink.

FISHING AND HUNTING

Like ourselves today, our ancestors needed to eat in order to sustain themselves. Unlike us, they could not simply stroll down to the local convenience shop and pick up a meal for dinner for very little money.

Most people in those days had to catch their own food. I have listed a few methods here that were used in Cavan.

Corry Fishing

This way of fishing is carried on by building a large *corry* on a river and allowing the water to flow away, thus leaving the bed of the river dry. The fish can be retrieved by hand.

Otter Fishing

A wooden cross is first built and a number of fly-casts are attached to it. It is then set floating on a lake. The fish, seeing the flies floating in the water, will jump at them and get caught in the same way as in bait fishing. Two or three fish at a time may be caught in this way.

Snare Fishing

A snare is made of rabbit wire and is attached to the end of a long rod. The snare is slipped over the fish's tail and up along its body. Then the fisherman gives a sudden pull to the rod and the fish may be drawn out of the water. The person fishing with a snare must have great skill, as the fish will swim away if it sees him approaching the water.

Snare Hunting

Snares are usually used for catching rabbits and hares. The snare is made of copper wire and a slender stick. First a loop is made at one end of the wire and the other end is attached to the stick. It is usually placed at the mouth of a rabbit burrow or on a rabbit or hare pass. When the rabbit or hare runs through, his body will be held there until the hunter comes along.

Pit Hunting

This method is usually practised in the bogs. A large round hole about 4ft deep and 18 inches in diameter is made. It is filled with water and covered over with light twigs and heather. When the hare runs across the hole, the twigs will break and it will drown.

Ferreting

First of all a ferret is procured. It is muzzled with strong cord and put into the burrow. The hunter puts a net at the mouth, in order to catch the rabbits, which run out before the ferret.

Bird Lime

First the hunter chooses a spot where he knows birds are prevalent. He brings with him some birdlime, which is a sticky substance made from boiled holly bark, and a bird in a cage; this bird is called a decoy bird. He places the cage in a convenient place and on each side of the cage he places some sticks to act as perches for the birds. These perches are well covered with lime. The decoy bird calls out and the other birds gather round it; when these birds perch on the sticks, their feathers get caught in the bird lime and they are held on the perches until the hunter comes. This method has also been practised for catching pheasants. A hoop was fixed in a large bag, which was plastered inside with birdlime. The pheasant's favourite food was placed in the bag and when the pheasant went into the bag to eat the food, his feathers stuck to the sides of the bag and it was held there until the hunter came.

CUSTOMS AT WEDDINGS, FUNERALS, AND WAKES

Customs and traditions are as much a part of the Irish psyche as are music and dance. Here are a few customs that were practised in Cavan.

Life and Love

Weddings are very happy occasions and can take place at any time of the year. There can, however, be a bit of an unusual rush around Shrove Tuesday as there was in the olden times. June and September are said to be particularly unlucky months for nuptials, whilst the ceremonies are generally held on Mondays, Tuesdays, or Wednesdays, as people are inclined to believe the old saying:

Monday for health,
Tuesday for wealth,
Wednesday the best day of all,
Thursday for losses,
Friday for crosses,
Saturday no day at all.

There is no mention of Sunday in this rhyme so no one ever hears of a marriage on a Sunday.

As is the case today, Cavan brides traditionally wore:

Something old,
Something new,
Something borrowed,
Something blue.

Often there is an old shoe thrown after the car to bring good luck.

A bride never returned to her own home until after the fourth Sunday in her new home and the newly married pair were not obliged to attend Mass on the first Sunday after their marriage.

Here is another old, and somewhat bizarre saying:

Change the name,
But not the letter,
Marry for worse,
Not for better.

An old rhyme regarding colours is:

Married in blue,
Your lover is true.
Married in black,
You are sure to come back.
Married in white,
You have chosen right.
Married in grey,
You will go far away.
Married in brown,
You will live out of town.
Married in yellow,
You'll be ashamed of the fellow.

Married in green,

Ashamed to be seen.

Married in grey,

You will rue the day.

In olden times, an oaten cake was broken on the bride's head when she came home after the ceremony. When the bridal couple were returning from the chapel, someone used to meet them with a bottle of whiskey and treat them and then break the bottle.

Death and Mourning

On a more sombre note, when a person in the house dies, all clocks are stopped and are not wound again until the corpse leaves the house.

Anyone going to a wake should bring a pipe full of tobacco home. Tobacco is supplied for the man and snuff for the women.

It is considered unlucky to leave a corpse alone; one should always have company.

If a corpse is not quite stiff when being put in the coffin it is supposed to be a sign that another death will take place in the family before long.

The person who washes and lays out a person should also place him in the coffin.

If the bed where the corpse was waked is at the back wall, the coffin should be brought out by the back door, and if near the front wall it should be taken out by the front door.

The 'feet end' of the coffin should come out of the house first and when the funeral reaches the graveyard the coffin should be turned so that the head faces west.

Four people of the same name as the corpse must take the remains from the house into the graveyard. The funeral should go by the longest route to the graveyard and the relatives should not take any shortcut coming home.

A person who meets a funeral on the road should walk back at least three steps and say a prayer.

Calendar Days

The Irish of yore lived their lives around the natural world, and the seasons dictated how they went about their business. The main calendar days that gave structure to their year were usually derived from the old pagan calendar and closely tied to how the world works.

Below are some of these festivals that were, and in many cases still are, mark in Cavan.

St Brigid's Day

St Brigid represents the Irish aspect of divine femininity in her role as patron of babies, blacksmiths, boatmen, cattle farmers, children whose parents are not married, children whose mothers are mistreated by the children's fathers, Clan Douglas, dairymaids, dairy workers, fugitives, Ireland, Leinster, mariners, midwives, milkmaids, nuns, poets, the poor, poultry farmers, poultry raisers, printing presses, sailors, scholars, travellers, and watermen. Here's a busy saint!

One folk tradition that continues in some homes on St Brigid's Day (or *Imbolc*) is that of Brigid's Bed. The girls and young, unmarried, women of the household or village create a corn dolly to represent Brigid, called the *Brideóg* ('little Brigid' or 'young Brigid'), adorning it with ribbons and baubles like shells or stones. They make a bed for the *Brideóg* to lie in.

On St Brigid's Eve (31st January), the girls and young women gather together in one house to stay up all night with the *Brideóg*, and are later visited by all the young men of the community, who must ask permission to enter the home, and then treat them and the corn dolly with respect.

Brigid is said to walk the earth on *Imbolc* eve. Before going to bed, each member of the household may leave a piece of clothing or strip of cloth outside for Brigid to bless. The head of the household will smother (or 'smoor') the fire and rake the ashes smooth. In the morning, they look for some kind of mark on the ashes, a sign that Brigid has passed that way in the night or morning. The clothes or strips of cloth are brought inside and are believed to now have powers of healing and protection.

Chalk Sunday

The first Sunday in Lent is known as Chalk Sunday, as it was the day when the custom was to mark an 'x' on the back of any boy or girl of marriageable age who had not yet been married. It was a common occurrence for the blackboard chalk in many local schools to go 'walkies' in the days leading up to this time.

This practice has largely fallen into disuse, and quite rightly too.

St Patrick's Day, 17 March

Our national saint's feast day was in former times a more solemn and pious celebration of his life. Pilgrimages were carried out and penance was done.

This, of course, was until the development of the custom of 'drowning the shamrock', which has come to the fore in the majority of places to get drunk on the saint's feast day.

Holy Thursday

This day is called Clipping Thursday. The nails and a lock of hair are clipped. The hair used to be hidden in a hole in the wall or under a stone.

Good Friday

Potatoes are set for a good crop.

A request made on Good Friday at three o'clock is supposed to be granted. Tradition also has it that a prayer said between one and three o'clock will release thirty-three souls from purgatory.

Easter Sunday

It is a custom to eat eggs and have picnics on Easter Morning and it is believed that the sun dances at six o'clock in the morning.

Whit Sunday

One should never sit or lie on the grass. Rumour has it that this causes a cold, and the person remains afflicted in some way forever afterwards. One should never bathe before Whit Sunday.

Whit Monday

It's regarded unlucky for any person or animal to be born on this day, and that they would at some point in the future be the cause of blood flowing. For this reason people sometimes make a baby born on this day squash a fly, or an animal to trample a chicken or bird in order to draw blood. Horses born on this day are especially unlucky. People believe that such a horse will be the cause of an accident in which a person will be killed.

May Day, 1 May

May Day was a day greatly associated with *pishogues*, and their connection with milk, butter, and cheese. In particular, it was on this day that the risk of having your farm produce stolen by malevolent forces was greatest. Livestock may actually fall ill on this day due to the interference of the *pishogue*.

It was generally understood that a common ass could not be affected by the shenanigans of the *pishogue*, for the simple reason that Our Lord was carried by an ass during his life on Earth, and the shape of the cross on the animal's back is testament to this.

It was also for this reason that it was seen as beneficial to have an ass on a farm to help protect the other animals on this day.

St John's Eve/Day, 23/24 June

This is bonfire night. Before leaving the fire, the mother – followed by the rest of the family – walks around the fire and recites three 'Our Fathers' and three 'Hail Marys' in honour of St John. The father then puts some of the coal in a bucket and drops one in the cornfield and potato field, among others; this is said to bring good luck to the crops.

St Stephen's Day, 26 December

On every St Stephen's Day, the wren boys go from house to house singing songs and gathering money. The song that is usually sung is 'The Wren'. Although not as common as in former times, it does still happen from time to time.

They dress in torn old clothes and blacken their faces. When they are finished collecting the money, they divide it equally among themselves. Some of them go to Cavan town to spend it.

The song they sing is:

The wren, the wren, the king of all birds
St Stephen's day she was caught it the furze!
Although she is little her honour is great
Get up young lady and give us a treat.
Dreolín, Dreolín, where is your nest
'Tis in the bush that I have best
'Tis in the holly and ivy tree, where all the boys follow me
I up with my stick and I knocked her down
An I brought her in to see the town

Up with the kettle and down with the pan
Give us our answer and let us begone.
Pockets of money and barrels of beer
And I wish ye all a happy new year.

New Year's Day, 1 January

One should never pay out money on this day. Water, dirty or clean, and ashes should not be thrown out. The floor should be brushed towards the hearth, not out on the door.

5

MYTHICAL CREATURES

FAIRY GOLD

One summer's week Seán found himself having a recurring dream. In this dream, Seán walked out of his cabin and over to the lone bush down in the bottom field. He took a spade to the roots of the tree and dug down to find an old black crock with gold coins inside.

After three days of exactly the same vision, Seán awoke and said to himself, 'Sure, I'm a poor man and could do with a bit of luck. I will be digging in that place on the eve of the next full moon to see what I can find.'

Why would he go digging in the evening, you might think. Well, you see, it was bad business to be disturbing any lone bush in the Irish countryside, for they were well known as being the abode of the wee people, and punishment for any interference with them would be brutal and severe. Surely everybody knows that, don't they?

Seán told nobody of his dreams nor of his intentions – to do so would be even more foolish than the act itself that he was about to carry out.

He took the spade from the byre and headed down to the *sceach*. Saying a quick *pater*, he drove it deep into the ground, severing a number of the ancient roots in the process. He felt a bit queasy for a short moment, but shrugged it off, blaming it on the excitement and a bit of questionable cabbage he had for his tea.

After digging for just a couple of minutes and before even breaking a sweat, the spade came to sudden halt with a dull thud. Not being the sound the strike off a stone would make, Seán got down on hands and knees and cleared away the dirt with his bare fingers. It not a stone; it was a fine big cast-iron crock, the kind they used to feed the people from during the time of the Famine, full to the brim with gold.

Seán dragged it out of the ground and, hoisting it up onto his broad shoulders, set out for home; staggering under the hefty load. He said to himself, 'Begorra, sure this must be a hundred weight if it's a day!' He thought about all the lovely things he could buy with the gold that was inside. It was so heavy that carrying it made him look like an aged and crippled man, bent over double, as he was.

When he came to his own place he went to the byre, and it was there that he put the crock down on the floor in front of the cows. Knowing that his wife had company in the house, he did not want to bring it inside in front of the neighbours for fear of their reaction to his sacrilege of the good people's tree, so he called her to the window and said, 'I have found a fine hoard of treasure with gold coins and precious jewels in it. All our troubles are over, so they are.' She was so excited with Seán's news that she feigned a dicky tummy and asked her guests to leave so that she could see for herself this hoard that he had told her of.

When the man and woman of the house were shot of the company they went out to the yard, and they were fair wild with delight. Seán told her the story of the three dreams and the finding of the crock of gold in under the roots of the lone bush. 'Did you spit on it?' she enquired of him. 'I did not, woman, so I didn't,' said he. With that she knew he had made a big mistake. She said,

'Sure isn't it is well known that fairy treasures are fierce enchanted and there is a power on them to melt away, but if a man were to spit on them that he'd get keeping it, surely.' On hearing this, Seán indeed realised that he had not done as he should have. It is true that women are wiser than men in such matters.

With that they quickly rushed into the byre and saw that the cows were terrified and trying to escape from the crock on the floor. 'Sure aren't they are in fierce dread of what's lying there in front of them,' said the wife, and she shrieked in terror when she saw that the crock was moving about on the floor of its own accord.

'Settle yourself, woman,' said Seán as he explained that it was probably a badger or fox that had sneaked into the byre.

'Turn over the crock and I will be praying aloud for protection, for it is surely no sound thing in it at all,' she said replied. With that he went over and turned over the hundredweight of treasure until he had it propped up against the hay bails. When he put his hand into the crock to see what was causing the fuss, a great eel looked out between his fingers. It had eyes on it the colour of flame and as blinding to the sight as the naked sun at noon of a summer's day.

With a cowardly yelp, the man gave such a leap of fright that it carried him to the door and there the paralysis of dread held him down. His wife let out a scream that could be heard in the next townland, if not the next parish, but she never dared to stir from where she was standing.

The eel twisted itself out of the crock and travelled along the ground, putting the six feet of its length into loops and knots. It climbed up a bail and, breaking through the thatch, was not seen again.

When Seán checked the crock, he saw that it was empty. His wife gave him a clout in the head and said, 'It is nothing but a fool ye are.' Neither of them ever had a day's luck after this sorry affair for the desecration of the lone bush.

The Shannon Pot

The Shannon Pot, or *Log na Sionna*, located near Dowra, is the recognised source of the mighty River Shannon, and at 386km long is the longest river in Ireland. Small streams high up in the Cuilcagh Mountains disappear into the limestone bedrock and join up together in mysterious underground caverns before breaking through to the deep brown reservoir, which is where the journey of this important and historic river begins.

Sionnan and the Ollphéist

Long before the dawn of time, there was a beautiful garden in the kingdom of Bréifne. In this garden was a magical well called *Tobar Segais*, or the Well of Wisdom. The only persons permitted to approach the well were druids.

There was a young girl who lived in a fort nearby. She was headstrong and irreverent of rules and regulations. This girl was called Sionnan, daughter of Lodan and granddaughter of the mighty Manannán Mac Lír, God of the Sea.

One day, Sionnan, bored of her own company, decided that it would be better craic to sneak into the forbidden garden to visit the well. She waited until the druids had left the area and tiptoed in through the gate. She crept through the ferns and flowers, around the hedge until she reached the large circular pool, bounded by the nine fabled hazel trees. Tiring of the 'disappointing' gardens, she began throwing pebbles into the well to entertain herself.

Fintan, the Salmon of Knowledge that resided in the well, was watching and became greatly angered by Sionnan's disrespect. He ordered the Ollphéist serpent to make things right, so the waters of the well began to rise quickly and began to overflow the area. Sionnan knew that something was wrong and began to retreat, but the waters pursued her, as did the Ollphéist that swam within. It chewed up the land in pursuance of Sionnan and the water filled the trenches left behind.

Finally the water consumed Sionnan and she was swept out to sea, where she drowned. For her affront, she was denied entrance into the Otherworld and was condemned to reside in the Shannon, which she created by her insolence. From that day forward she would be known as the Queen of the Well Spirits.

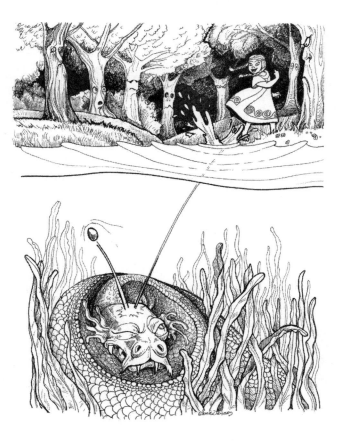

The Salmon of Knowledge

Long ago when Fionn MacCumhaill – the great leader of the Fianna – was still a young boy, he was sent to live with a man named Finnegas. Now, Finnegas was a very wise and learned man; a poet, scholar, and composer, who knew most things. He knew more about the earth and stars than any other man in Ireland; in fact, so learned was he that he was known by everybody as Finnegas the Wise.

It was because of the old man's vast knowledge that Fionn was sent to him and in return for an education, Fionn would assist Finnegas with various chores around the house and farm.

There was one thing that troubled Finnegas greatly, and that was despite all he knew, he still did not know everything that there was to know in the world. He was aware of the magical salmon of knowledge known as Fintan, who lived in the dark mysterious well that gave birth to the sacred Shannon. Around this grew nine sacred hazel trees, which flowered, seeded, and fruited all at the same time. Fintan the salmon ate of its fruit, which gave it the knowledge of all the world and it was said that anybody who ate of the fish would gain this knowledge. Finnegas had cast his rod into the pot for seven long years in an attempt to catch the salmon and gain its knowledge, but never managed to get it to take the bait.

On one particular day, Finnegas was sitting with Fionn at the pot and they were discussing the world when all of a sudden he felt a tug on his fishing line. He grabbed it quickly and felt a great struggle at the other end. Fionn helped him and together they reeled the mighty salmon onto land, and waited until it breathed its last breath. Realising his dream had finally come true, Finnegas said he needed to sit and gather his thoughts for a while, so he asked Fionn to take the fish home and cook it for his supper but he gave him strict instructions not to eat any.

Fionn went home and put the fish into the pan, turning it several times to ensure that it would be evenly cooked for his master. Whilst the fish fried away, Fionn noticed a large blister rising on its skin and, letting curiosity get the better of him, reached out to burst it but in doing so, the boiling fat splashed all over his thumb, severely burning it. Shrieking with the pain, he immediately put his thumb in his mouth to soothe the burn and soon began to see visions of the world.

On his return from the Shannon Pot, Finnegas asked Fionn how his supper was coming along and, noticing an unusual silence, looked in his eyes. On seeing that his eyes shone with a previously unseen wisdom, Finnegas asked if he had eaten any of the fish. Fionn said that he had not, but explained the blister incident. Finnegas then dismissed Fionn from his service, as there was nothing left for him to learn in either this life or the next.

Having gained all the knowledge of the world, Fionn was to rise through the ranks and lead the mighty Fianna. To draw on the knowledge he had gained, he merely had to bite on his thumb and the visions would flow to him.

THE *DOBHARCHÚ* OF LOUGH SHEELIN

There are many stories told of fierce animals that lived in Ireland long ago. One of the most strange and sorrowful incidences ever told is connected with the *Dobharchú*, a fearsome cross between a phantom hound and an otter. There are many different but similar versions of this tale, but the one we are concerned with is that from Lough Sheelin.

The story is told that about 300 years ago, a woman named McLoughlin went to the lakeshore to wash the clothes of her family. Realising that she had been down by the shore for longer

than would be normal, her husband went out the door and called to her but, on hearing no response, went to investigate. To his great distress, he found her stone dead and covered in blood. Not only this, though: there was also with a strange animal lying on top of her dead body, and it was hissing away. Filled with terror and grief, he ran back to his house and got his sword to put the beast to death. He came back and sliced the head off the animal, but as it died, it let a horrific and strange whistling cry.

At the same time, another animal of the same kind came out from the lake at speed and chased the man. Fearing for his own life, he ran as fast as he could but was still able to fetch his brother along the way and two horses. They galloped away, and the beast was still in pursuit. At a turn in the road, the *dobharchú* got hold of one of the horses and devoured it in one go, luckily without the man. They made it over the border to Leitrim and, on entering a graveyard, tipped over a headstone; when the beast followed behind, the stone fell on its head and killed it.

They decided to bury the poor woman in this graveyard and a surviving headstone commemorates this event to this day.

THE *POOKA* OF CUILCAGH

Mary lived with her father Pat Tom in a little shack built into a bank of earth in the townland of Dunmakeever on the western slopes of Cuilcagh Mountain. With their little comfortable home, Jess, their grey-speckled horse, and a few cows, they lived a simple life and were content with their lot.

One summer's evening, Mary took her crook and went out to check on the cows up on the mountain, a task that was part of her usual routine of an evening. The mountain of Cuilcagh is a wild and rugged crag, and ascending it can be a challenge on the best of days.

She started out and with the fine hot evening that it was, she quickly got tired and sat down on a slab of rock to have a wee rest. All of a sudden, she saw their horse Jess come out from behind a lone bush and stroll up to her. 'Why are you this far up the mountain, lad?' she asked. Now, of course she was not expecting the horse to answer her, so she stood and mounted him, thinking that she could save her legs by riding up to check on the cows. She gave a gentle 'hup!' and off they went up the mountain.

Mary thought Jess's temperament seemed a little bit different somehow but couldn't quite put her finger on how. Soon the horse started to trot without so much as a warning, and before Mary knew it, he sped up to a gallop. In fact, so fast was he going that she was certain that they were no longer on the ground and she could only hold onto his mane for dear life. No amount of 'whoas' could slow or halt the horse. She looked down at his back, and no longer was it speckled-grey; it was jet-black and when the horse looked up at her, she saw that its eyes were fiery red. No longer was this their faithful Jess! To her horror, she realised that she was sitting on the back of a *Pooka*.

They continued to ascend the mighty Cuilcagh when she saw other fairy horses join them, and on one of them was an aunt of hers who had passed away the previous year. 'Stay quiet, my dear Mary, and eat or drink nothing that is given to you,' said she.

The *pooka* continued to gallop up the mountain until suddenly they came to a ring of stones with a thorn growing in the centre that Mary had not noticed before. The *pooka* took a standing leap into the centre of the ring and they found themselves inside a vast cavern in the earth. The *pooka* continued with the young girl on its back and only let her off when they came to a grand castle; from outside she could hear all kinds of music, singing, and general merriment. Mary went in and was greeted by Queen Sadhbh of the good folk, who was very kind to her and told her that they would return her to her home once they had shown her some hospitality. Mary sat down at a long table and butlers set out huge platters of the finest food and drink that she had ever seen. She was so hungry and thirsty after riding for hours on end, but remembered what his aunt had said. 'Aren't you going to have some food, young *cailín*?' said the queen.

'Aye, I am just resting after my journey before I have some of your delicious food,' said Mary, trying to think of how to make her escape. 'Have something to drink, then, to quench your thirst at

least,' insisted the queen. 'I will in a moment, your highness,' said Mary.

Mary waited and waited and kept making her excuses every time and soon she began to find herself becoming weary and falling asleep. Very soon the urge was too great to resist and she could no longer stay awake, despite the loud music, dancing, and singing. She suddenly dropped off into a slumber. Slumping forward, her head hit the table. This made her wake suddenly, and on waking up she saw that she was sitting at the table in her home. No longer was she tired, hungry, or thirsty; she was fresh as a daisy. She went outside to check that everything was as it should be, and indeed everything was as it was before she set out to check on the cows.

THE WAILING BANSHEE OF THE MCCABES

Many Irish people will be familiar with the tale of the banshee. From the Irish *bean sídhe*, meaning fairy woman, she is a spirit who is said to forewarn of a death of a family member. She usually, but not always, appears to the members of clans whose surnames contain the prefix Mac, or Ó. Some believe that she is the ghost of a young woman who was brutally killed and died so horribly that her spirit is left to wander the world, watching her family and loved ones and warning them when a violent death is imminent.

During the time of mass emigration and 'American wakes', many of the nation's children could not emigrate fast enough to make a life on the other side of the Atlantic. Young Margaret McCabe was only 12 years old when her time came to board the transatlantic ship bound for the Canadian coast. She was an only child of a small branch of the McCabes and her parents could only scrape enough money together for her fare, meaning that they would stay behind to look after the farm.

They had a send off for her at the quay the night before, as did so many others, and the ship, called the *Fionnuala*, set out promptly on time at dawn the following day. Margaret's parents were initially concerned at the huge number of people who appeared to be on the ship, but shrugged it off, thinking that it was just down to the hugely emotional day that was in it.

The departure of Margaret hit her parents hard, but seemed to distress her father considerably. When they were home, he was in the mood to be alone and went for a walk across the field to the little lake. He saw something in the corner of his eye and it appeared to be an old woman combing her hair down by the lake. 'There are no mass paths here; who is this woman?' he thought to himself so he went down and asked her what she was doing.

When he got there, she turned around and he could see that she was a horrific looking creature, dressed in old rags with long white hair, red eyes, and pointed, rotten teeth. She began wailing and shrieking, and water began to pour from her mouth. He turned around and ran as quickly as he could back to the house to get away from the awful sight.

He told his wife what he had seen but she had not heard anything so that night they went to bed as usual at dusk, but they were both kept up all night by the wailing of the spirit. The wife knew at once that this was no ordinary spirit; it was their family's banshee and this greatly concerned her.

They arose at first light and heard a knock at the door. It was a policeman who carried a telegram. They opened it and it read:

Transatlantic ship 'Fionnuala' has foundered. All lives lost.

They had lost their precious Margaret and it was the banshee who was forewarning of her impending death.

The Royal Palace of the
Three Counties

On a forgotten road somewhere near the meeting point of the borders of Cavan, Leitrim, and Fermanagh lies a secret palace. This palace is only visible to some sensitive people, and only in certain lights and at certain times. This fine building is no ordinary palace but is said to be one of the royal seats of the wee people of Ulster.

One day and without warning, when the fairy prince Iarla was literally knee-high to a grasshopper, he mysteriously vanished. As everybody knows, the wee folk are known for their mischievous ways, but even this was unusual for a fairy child. Distraught with worry, the king sent all his staff out to search for his only son and heir in every known place of his kingdom. They searched high and they searched low, but nobody could find him nor find out what had happened to him.

Despite the offers of huge rewards for his safe return, no sign or sound of Prince Iarla was ever found and, needless to say, the royal parents were beyond consolation.

Years passed and there was not a day went by when they did not think of their little boy, but they had to resign themselves to the fact that he was gone.

One summer's evening, a young local lad was walking along the back roads of the area. He was deep in thought when out of the corner of his eye he thought he saw a gold castle, but shrugged it off as a trick of the dusk light and continued on his way. He thought that he'd have a wee rest and lay down on the grassy bank beside the road but he soon nodded off. He had a dream that he saw a young fairy lad on hands and knees, scrubbing the flags of a kitchen floor. This was a very tired and overworked Prince Iarla. The prince bade the boy to approach, and said, 'I have been taken from my family by the evil king of the giants and has he made me his servant. For seven long years have I toiled in his castle under the cairn above yonder.'

The young lad was confused by what he was seeing and hearing. 'Indeed I am sorry for your plight, Sir, but what is it that I can do for you? I am only a poor farmer's son,' said the lad.

'It is releasing me tonight, you'll be, and I'll be making sure that you are rewarded for your service.'

'How am I to know that this is for real?' said the lad, and with that the prince gave him all the proof he needed. Saying, 'Take this as your sign!' he threw his scrubbing brush at the lad, hitting him square in the forehead. Well I can tell you, the lad thought his brain would fall out with the force of it. Uttering a curse or two, he yelped with the shock and pain. He woke up at the side of the road where he had fallen asleep and, on putting his hand to his forehead, felt the great bump left by the brush.

The young lad was well acquainted with the neighbouring countryside and was familiar enough with the cairn that the prince had told him of. It was up on a small hill and surrounded by rush-covered marshes.

Such was the impression that the dream made on the lad that he was determined to see what truth was in it and so decided to embark on a wee adventure to the cairn to find out for himself. On his way he called into Tommy, the local blacksmith, to borrow a clump of iron, for it is well known that the fairies have a disliking of the stuff; this would be his insurance if things went badly for him. When Tommy heard of the lad's dream, he promised to help him and offered to drive him up the hill on his donkey cart.

They had a hearty supper of smoked eel and potatoes and then Tommy harnessed the donkey for the trip ahead. The sun was just going down when they set off, but they noticed that it was one of the most beautiful sunsets they had ever seen. They soon got to the base of the cairn and Tommy bade the lad farewell, telling him that he would be waiting for him there when he returned.

The lad was extremely anxious as he ascended the cairn and looked for the entrance to the giant's castle. Just as he was about to give up, he saw a glimmer of light from among a couple of stones around the top. He pulled these away to reveal a stunning marble staircase. With his iron in his kitbag, he descended, with his heart nearly beating right out of his chest. The lad descended deeper and deeper, into the cairn itself, and soon enough the moonlight outside was a dim and distant memory. His fear grew and he thought that he would not make it out alive. He followed the tunnel that led him to a light, and when he got to the end he saw a large room lit by a single, solitary candle on the floor. The only piece of furniture in the room was a massive chair and in it was sitting a very large bearded man, snoring. 'This must be the king of the giants,' thought the lad and with a tremble in his voice he announced, 'I am here to claim the Prince Iarla.'

The giant awoke with a jolt and, shaking the dust off himself, stood up in anger. 'Who dares enter my castle and what do you seek?' Again, the lad announced, 'I am here to claim the Prince Iarla.'

'And who had the audacity to send you here?' said the giant. 'It was of my own accord that I came, your highness,' said the brave lad.

'Then, if it is for the prince you have come, it is the prince you shall have,' and with that the giant led the lad through a big steel door in the corner of the room and down a further flight of steps to where the kitchens were located. 'LINE UP!' shouted the giant to the servants working in the lower regions of the castle, and after they did, the giant said to the lad, 'Now choose your prince, lad, and make sure you choose the right one, for if you do not choose correctly, you will join their ranks and toil here until your dying day.'

The lad was more than a little confused, as there were hundreds upon hundreds of servants, all looking similar and dressed in identical uniforms. He could only half remember what the young prince looked like but he paid close attention and looked at each one's features in the hope that he would recognise the prince, but it was a lot more difficult than he thought.

He took the iron out of his pocket and threw it down onto the giant's foot. He let a massive yelp out of him that echoed throughout the whole castle, and fell to the floor crying in pain and grasping his throbbing toes. With that, Prince Iarla came forward and took the lad's hand and made for the exit. On seeing the two escaping, the giant let out a huge roar of anger but this unsettled the cairn under which the castle was built and rocks began to fall in through the ceilings and corridors. Just as the two boys got safely out, the cairn collapsed in on itself and that was the end of the evil king of the giants.

Prince Iarla hugged the lad and thanked him for all he had done to free him. 'You must come back to my palace for a feast for I have not been seen for some seven long years.' With that they met Tommy the blacksmith, who carried them in his donkey cart out to the back roads where the fairy palace was. When they rounded the hill, Iarla clicked his fingers and the finest golden palace ever seen suddenly appeared. The royal pages saw the three approaching and summoned the king and queen, telling them that Prince Iarla was returning.

The royal parents rushed out and, scarcely believing their eyes, hugged and kissed their son, vowing to never let him go again. They had a mighty feast and *hooley* to celebrate his return that lasted throughout the night with the music being heard all over the countryside.

THE GHOST OF CABRA CASTLE

The original Cabra Castle was situated not far from Cromwell's Bridge within the present-day forest park of Dun na Rí in Kingscourt.

Although some ruins of the castle do remain, they are very scant and scattered. It is believed that the castle and lands formed part of an earlier fortress and was the stronghold of the O'Reilly clan until it was confiscated on Cromwell's orders in the mid-seventeenth century.

It was during the closing years of the eighteenth century that the Pratt family were in possession of this building when a great injustice occurred.

There were two sons and a daughter in the family, and one of the sons fell deeply and passionately in love with a servant girl by the name of Sarah. In the strong class-based society that existed at the time, this was not the done thing at all and would not be tolerated by the senior members of the family. Despite this, the young couple continued to profess their love, but they had to do it in secrecy.

They knew all parts of the wooded area and were able to take walks in the evening and the odd picnic in peace away from the glare of the upper and lower classes. They expressed their love for each other constantly and if it were not for the differences in class and religion, they would already be married.

One day, Sarah woke up and felt a little different from the usual; she could not exactly describe what it was but she knew that she should seek some advice and so went to talk to the head servant, Mrs Burke. After a while, Mrs Burke let out a shriek. 'Well, isn't it only pregnant you're after getting yourself!' and with that she gave Sarah a smack of the hand across her face. 'And who, might I ask, is the father?' said Mrs Burke. 'It is the Master Pratt,' said Sarah.

'The Lord a' mercy on us. A Protestant! A Protestant!' Mrs Burke reefed the young servant by the hair and ordered her to her quarters while she decided what was to be done.

Mrs Burke called a meeting with the lady of the house and discussed the situation with her, and then she discussed it with the man of the house. Now that the secret was out that the young servant girl had become pregnant by the landlord's son, the family decided that they could not bear the scandal that would arise from such a situation.

During the night, Sarah was awoken by the sound of somebody at her door, and suddenly the door was forced open with a crash and there stood five of the landlord's men. They put a sack over Sarah's head and bundled her into an old cart, which they pulled by hand. They brought her deep into the forest and when they got to the one of the old bridges, they tied a noose around her neck and flung her over the bridge to hang until she was dead.

Truly, a gruesome and horrific ending.

The bridge survives to this day and is known as Sarah's Bridge. A nearby well is also given the name of Sarah's Well or Tobar Sorcha. Cabra Castle is now a five-star, twenty-four-bedroom hotel, and the former servants' quarters are now known as the courtyard accommodation.

It is said that in the dead of the night, the haunting cries of a baby may still be heard in and all around the estate of Cabra Castle and local people believe that it is the sound of the baby still pining for its mother. It is also said that Sarah's lost soul still wanders the castle in search of her love and her unborn child. A spectre has been seen by many people over the years.

I hope that one day poor Sarah and her wee baby will find rest for the evil that was done to them.

How to Catch a Leprechaun

Folklore surrounding the Irish leprechaun has survived hundreds if not thousands of years, with various stories being passed down through the generations. At one point, everybody knew somebody who had had an encounter with a leprechaun, but sadly these days such encounters appear to be getting rarer and rarer. This could either be because leprechauns are less common in recent times or have become better at avoiding contact with people.

From the Irish meaning 'small body', the leprechaun is a working man from the realm of the fairies, believed to be the only one with a trade – that of shoemaking. Each leprechaun is said to have a pot of gold, which they hide deep in the countryside, but more commonly at the end of the rainbow. So devious are these little fellows that they will do anything to escape from man so they should never be trusted. They tend to dislike humans, who always seem to chase them for free wishes and free gold.

It is often said that if you spot a leprechaun you might be better off to take no notice, as the difficulty you can end up in afterwards can be much more trouble than it's worth. Unfortunately, with cities in Ireland expanding, the poor wee leprechauns are being driven further underground away from man, and taking their rainbows (and gold) with them.

If you get lucky and manage to catch a leprechaun, you need to hold him by the ankle and be smarter than him, otherwise he will vanish right from your hands. If he is held tight, he is bound by oath to grant three wishes to his captor or to lead them to his pot of gold coins.

It is wise, however, to be cautious with a leprechaun and always know that they are masters at deception. Many a person who thought they could outsmart an Irish leprechaun and had selected the three wishes would either go insane trying to think of what to wish for or have their wishes backfire with something bad happening.

MARRIAGE OF THE MERROW

Once upon a time, there lived a man in a little house beside the sea. He made his money by crafting small figures from the shells he collected on shore, and on one particular day as he was out collecting the shells he saw a merrow sitting on a half-submerged rock. She had greenish/blue hair and he noticed that she was stroking it whilst whistling to herself.

He hid from view and sneaked up to her among the woods that grew down to the water on one side. When he was right up behind her, he nabbed her and ripped her *cochallin draíochta* or little magic hood off her head, and in doing so turned her into a normal woman and made her a slave.

He knew that as long as he had her *cochallin draíochta*, she would be unable to return to the water and so she lived for years with him and bore him five children, who were fully human apart from having scaly skin and webbed fingers and toes. The man hid her hood in between the eaves just under the thatch.

When their children were grown up, the merrow asked the eldest if he had seen her hood, and, not realising its importance, he told her that he had seen it in the thatch. With that, she rose from the kitchen table and seized it, putting it back on to her head. As she did this, her hair turned green, her skin scaly, and her legs merged together, forming a tail. She fell to the floor and slid out the door and down to the shore. Giving one last look back at her family, she shot into the water and was never seen again.

The Mermaid and the Princess

Once upon a time, there was a king who had three sons. Two were very good workers, whilst the other was the rake of the family. The father put him away from the castle and he went around wandering through the woods and on to the next land. In the woods he saw a king and his daughter hunting for wild animals, although the daughter was wandering away from the hunt and further into the woods. The rake watched her stop under a particularly big tree. There was a big wolf high up in the trees and was just about to jump on her, so the rake pulled out his pistol and fired a shot at the wolf, hitting him square in the forehead and killing him stone dead. The king, who had seen what had happened, went over to the rake, thanked him for saving his daughter's life, and offered his daughter's hand in marriage as his reward. The king brought the young couple to the chapel in his castle and they both got married and lived very happily together.

One day, the couple were down at the seaside and the princess strayed away from the prince. As he followed her, he saw a mermaid come on to the shore, and he watched as she caught the princess by the foot and dragged her into the murky waters of the lake. The prince rushed over as quickly as he could but could not save her. He went home crying, and the king saw him and asked, 'What is wrong with you?'

'A mermaid brought away my wife and I could not get near her.'

When the king heard this, he didn't know what to do. The next day the prince went down to the shore to see if he could get her back, and he saw a little woman selling rock and sweets. 'What is wrong with you, my good man?' she asked.

'My wife was taken away by the mermaid yesterday and I can't get her,' he replied.

'Well,' said the little woman, 'you come down to this shore today at one o'clock and begin to fry rashers and eggs. When the mermaid smells them she will come to the shore. When you see her, grab her and do not let her go until she returns your wife.'

The prince went home and told the king what he had heard, so both he and the king went to the shore at one o'clock and fried up the rashers and eggs as instructed, all the while keeping watch for the mermaid. When the mermaid finally appeared and cautiously came out of the water, the prince lept at her and forcefully held her, but she was far too strong and returned to the lake and dragged the prince in with her. The king was shocked beyond reason with what he saw and he did not know what to do.

Day after day, the king would go down to the shore and wondered how he could get them back but there was no sign of them. In the meantime, the prince was brought to the same place that the princess was taken, and they were always plotting how they would get away. There was a little dwarf living in the mermaid's castle and they asked him how they could get away out of the castle. He told them that when he would get the mermaid gone away, he would tell them. After a while, the mermaid went up to the shore looking for people. Then the dwarf said, 'I will turn ye into two birds, because she likes birds.' So with that, he turned them into birds and let them up to the top of the water. He put a little wand under one of their wings and told them that when they reached the shore, they were to tap themselves with it and they would return to man and woman.

They did this when they got on to the shore, and when they went home there was a great welcome for them and they put the kettle on and had a cup of tae to celebrate.

6

MAGICAL HAPPENINGS

THE FAST SPRINTER

Long ago there lived a gentleman who had two daughters, named Tara and Aoife, and one son, named Rory.

Miles away there was a very big mountain with a beautiful castle hidden away among the woods.

The gentleman realised that he was getting on in age and wanted to provide for his daughters, and so he called firstly his son, who was a very fast runner, and said to him that he should go off and seek his fortune. His son replied that he would not do so until his two sisters were settled, and that he would remain with his father until that happened.

Another day the father called Rory and his sisters and told them that there was to be a race up the mountain and whoever won this race would get the castle that was on the mountain. Early next morning, the three siblings got up and started off. Rory sprinted up the mountain and reached the top in no more than a few minutes. So fast was he that his sisters thought he had got lost, so they turned around and went home to tell their father.

Rory wasn't lost; instead, as he was tired after all that running, he had sat down under a tree. After a while he saw a dim light and saw doors open; soon, a beautiful lady came before him, riding a white horse. She said he had won her castle and he should marry her. Rory replied that he would first see his father about it and the lady agreed, offering him a horse to take him home. He refused, saying that he would go home the same way that he came.

He reached his father's house and told him all about the castle and the woman he had met at the tree on the top. His father thought that there may be some fairy magic at play and so told him that he should complete the race one more time and that this time his two sisters would get two horses to help them keep up with him. Unfortunately, as they were riding up the mountain, they both fell off and into a river. After a wee while a man came along with a wand and hit them with it, and when he did they were once more on the horses. Being confused and disorientated, they decided to return home and they told their father that it was their brother who assaulted them.

When the boy came home, the father gave him a crock of gold and, bizarrely, declared that he was to be beheaded. Not wanting to hang around for to lose his head, the boy ran away from his father and could not be found.

A few days later, there was to be another race to the mountain and he, his two sisters, and many others were there. The beautiful lady declared she would choose one of the competitors for her husband. She passed every one of them until she saw Rory, whom she chose. The two sisters lived with their father and, not wanting to only be defined by being married, first made their own way in the world before marrying and seeing out their days in blissful happiness.

MICHAEL AND THE HAUNTED HOUSE

Long ago there lived a man named Michael, who – along with his wife Kitty and their seven children – dwelt in a wee cottage near

Cootehill. The poor family, God be good to them, did not have a shilling to their name and they were starving with hunger.

One day, Michael said to himself that he would need to go out and get work if he wanted to better his lot and that of his long-suffering family. He met a man on the road and asked him if he knew anywhere he could find work. The man told him that the local lord would give five pounds to anybody who would stay one night in the haunted house on the hill. Michael promptly went to the lord and agreed to take on the bet.

That night, Michael kissed his wife and children goodnight and went to stay in the haunted house. He opened the big creaking front door, walked into the parlour and lit the fire before settling down for the evening in the big armchair placed at the hearth. He thought to himself that this wasn't too bad at all.

Whilst in the space of half waking and half sleeping, Michael became aware of the sound of a man entering the room and standing between him and the fireplace. Without saying anything, the man left some time later.

The following morning, the lord unlocked the front door and let Michael out, asking him what he had seen during the night. Michael said that he had not seen anything at all.

The lord offered him a further five pounds to stay a second night, and Michael jumped at the chance, thinking that it was easy money to be had. The second night passed just as the first night did, and the lord was so impressed that he asked Michael to stay a third night, which he duly did.

On this night, the visitor turned and said to him, 'I am the ghost of the king's father and he will give you fifteen pounds tomorrow for your bravery. You are the first man to have stayed here for one night, never mind three. The other two died of fright when they saw me. Here is a pot of gold and a magic tablecloth. When you spread out the tablecloth, everything that you wish to eat will be laid out on it. Go out and hide them in a safe place until the morning.' On saying this, the ghost suddenly disappeared, and Michael went out and carried out the spectre's instructions.

In the morning, the lord paid Michael the money as agreed and he left, retrieving the gold and tablecloth on his way home.

On the road, he met a tinker. The tinker told Michael that he was starving and so Michael, being the generous soul that he was, unrolled the tablecloth and the tinker sat down and filled his belly with the finest of foods. He was so grateful that he gave Michael the gift of a sack and told him that if ever he was in danger to open the sack and to release the army that was contained within.

Michael picked up the gold, the tablecloth, and the sack and went home. His wife greeted him at the gate, kissed him, and told him how nice the neighbours had been to them whilst he was away. She suggested that they should invite them in for dinner to thank them.

Michael threw the grandest of parties. When the proceedings were over, all the neighbours went home and told everybody about the great tablecloth that Michael and Kitty had. The lord in turn heard of this tablecloth and decided that he must have it, so he sent his soldiers to go and get it.

Michael saw the soldiers approaching and opened the sack given to him by the tinker, and out marched his own army. When the two armies met there was a great battle between them. Needless to say, Michael's army won. Michael went home and put his army into the sack once more.

He had a new house built and got his children into college. Both he and Kitty lived and loved happily ever afterwards.

The Greedy Fox

There was a woman in Killeshandra, the wife of a fisherman. She was always lucky and they were never short of fish; so much so that they were able to store some away in the house ready for market.

To her great annoyance, a fox took to the habit of coming in at night and devouring all the best and finest fish. She went out into the woods and got a big stick and kept it beside the hearth, determined to keep watch for the scavenger.

One day, as she and her daughter were knitting in the kitchen, the house suddenly became quite dark. The door was flung open as if by the blast of a tempest, and in strutted a huge copper-coloured fox. He went straight up to the fire, turned round and growled at them.

'Why, surely this is foxy,' said the young daughter, who was busy sorting the fish. 'I will teach you reverence,' said the fox, and with that, jumped at her, scratching her neck and arm until he drew blood.

'That is your punishment,' said he, 'and I'll thank you to be more civil whenever a gentleman comes to visit you.' And with that he walked over to the door and shut it closed to prevent any of them going out, for the poor young girl had made a desperate rush to get away.

Just then a man was going by, and on hearing the cries, tried frantically to push the door open to get in and help, but the fox stood on the threshold and would let no one pass. The man attacked him with his blackthorn, giving him a sound blow to the side of the head. The fox, however, was more than a match in the fight and flew at him, tearing at his face and hands so badly that the man at last took to his heels and ran away as fast as he could.

'Now, it is time for my dinner,' said the fox, going up to examine the fish that was laid out on the tables. 'I hope the fish is good today. Now, don't disturb me, nor make a fuss. I will help myself.' With that he jumped up, and began to devour all the best fish, whilst he growled at the woman.

'Go away out of that, you furry beast,' she cried, giving it a blow with the tongs, but the fox only grinned, and went on tearing and spoiling and devouring the fish, evidently not a bit the worse for the blow. With this, both the woman and girl attacked it with sticks, and struck hard blows, they thought. But the fox glared at them and, making a leap, tore at their heads and arms till the blood came, and they both ran shrieking from the house.

Later, the mistress returned, carrying with her a bottle of holy water. Looking in, she saw the fox still devouring the fish, and not minding. So she crept over quietly and threw the water on it without a word. No sooner was this done than a dense black smoke filled the place. Nothing was seen but the two eyes of the fox, and they were burning like coals of fire. But when the smoke gradually cleared and disappeared, the fox had run away.

From that time the fish remained untouched and safe from harm, and the greedy fox was seen no more.

Araild and the Card Game

There was once a king and a queen and they were fairly well off, as royalty often are. Now, this fancy royal pair subscribed to the mantra of 'if you've got it, flaunt it', and so fond were they of this that they regularly held grand suppers and dances in the castle for their friends.

The king and queen were not the best at the aul' bookkeeping, so they never kept an eye on the pennies, as they had never needed to. One day they got into a bit of a fluster when their banker called to the castle with beads of cold sweat on his brow and a shake in his voice. He said, 'Your majesties, I don't know how to tell you this, so I don't, but you are flat broke.' Never before had the royals heard these words and when the reality of their seriousness sank in, they broke down in tears, wondering whatever they would do, and what their friends would think.

The royals had a young son, Prince Araild, who passed his time doing nothing else but reading book upon book. The king would often mock him, saying, 'You should enjoy your inheritance and not pass your time with such folly!' but Araild ignored him and continued with his head between the pages.

One day, Araild read in one of his books that if he went to the shore every day for a year and a day, he would get a fortune. Overhearing the predicament the family were in, he thought that he would give this a try, so off he went with his books and sat by the shore every day. The days flew by and in no time at all, a whole year had passed. It was on the last day of his visits, when the family had run out of food entirely, so he had to go fasting. He sat down by the shore with a rumble in his tummy.

Suddenly, he saw a ship pass around the headland and a wee boat row to shore from it. It pulled up on the strand beside him and a short tubby man got out of it. 'You, lad! What are you doing there?' said he. Araild told him of the book he read and of the prophecy. 'Would you play a game of cards with me, lad?' said the man. 'Surely I will,' said the prince.

'Tell me this, lad. What wish does your heart desire?'

'I would wish for the castle rooms to be filled with gold and silver, and for the empty kitchens to be full of food once more.' So, it was that the boy won that game and his prize was granted. They decided to have another game and the old man declared that he wanted to have his home out there beyond at the end of the world. The old man won this game and his prize was also waiting for him.

The boy went home to his mother for to get his dinner but she said, 'Araild, the situation is as it was this morning; there is not even a *crumpeen* of bread in the whole place.' Araild replied, 'Ah, but have a look in the kitchens and tell me if this is still the situation.' The queen did as he instructed, and to her amazement, every press and cupboard in the place was full to the brim with the finest of foods and drinks. 'Now take a look in the other rooms,' said the prince, and sure enough, they were filled from floor to ceiling with the shiniest of gold and silver. The queen was in ecstasy and shouted with glee, 'All our troubles are over!'

THE HARE AND THE OLD WOMAN

There was a strong farmer and he had nine beautiful cows, all grazing on the best of land. Surely that was a great prosperity, and you'd be thinking him the richest man in all of Cavan. But he only got a little milk from his nine lovely cows, and he could get no butter from that milk.

They'd be churning in that house for three hours or maybe for five hours of a morning, and at the end of it only a few wee grains of butter is all they'd be rewarded with – the size of which would be no bigger than a robin's eggs floating on the top of the milk. Even that much did not remain to it, for when his wife ran the strainer in under them, they melted from the churn.

There were great confabulations held about the loss of the yield, but the strength of the spoken word was powerless to restore what was gone. Herself began to think that himself had been struck down with the evil eye, and it was overlooking his own cattle; he was by walking through them and fasting at the dawn of day. The notion didn't please him too well; indeed he was horrid vexed at her for saying the like, but he went no more among the cows until after his breakfast time. Sure that did no good at all – the milk yield continued to dwindle each day. With butter selling at a lovely price in the market, it was irksome to have none to sell.

The man of the house went out walking with his dog that evening and, to their utter shock, they saw a hare running with the nine cows through the field. The hound took off after the hare and followed it through the quicken hedge, over the ditches, and down past the lake. The farmer remembered a story his father told him about hares being enchanted people. He said to himself, 'I don't know if is true or not, but there's something not quite right about these things.'

There was a small, wee house up an old *boreen*, and that was where the hunt headed for. The hare ran up the lane not a yard in front of the hound, and she made a leap to get into the cabin by a wee hole in the wall. The hound got a grip of her and took a chunk out of her side before she disappeared into the hole. The farmer pulled open the door and ran inside the old derelict shack, looking around for the injured hare. Both he and the hound heard some rustling in the next room, and with that pushed into the kitchen. There was neither sight nor sign of a hare to be found, but an old woman lay in a corner, bleeding. The dog gave out an awful whine and pushed his nose into his master's feet.

The farmer then turned and left for home, saying, 'Surely there's not a many in the world do be hunting hares through the fields and catching old women bleeding to death.' On reaching his front gate, herself came running out shouting with glee, 'Will you look at the gallons of beautiful milk the cows are after giving this day?' And sure enough, from that day to this, there was a great plenty of milk and a right yield of butter on the churn.

THE DRAGON

One time there was a widow who had a son and two daughters. The eldest child, the son, said he would go out to seek his fortune and make a better life for himself. He started off the next day and travelled a very long road until he came to a farmer. The farmer, liking the cut of his jib, employed him and sent him to work beside a high wall. He told him not to look over the wall as there was enchanted ground on the other side and it would not do him well to see what is to be seen.

One day when the farmer was away, the boy's curiosity got the better of him and he thought that if no one knew then there would be no harm in taking a wee look over the wall. Up he got and piled some boxes up against the wall to climb up and take a peek. To his amazement and wonder, he saw the finest of castles that ever there was to be seen. Allowing his curiosity to go one step further, he threw one leg over the wall and then the second, and with a sudden leap he was down on the other side of the wall in the enchanted land.

He saw an old woman come running towards him and shouting, 'What brought you here, young man?'

'I looked over the wall and when I saw such beauty, I came over to see what it was like', said he.

Seeing that the *gosoon* was no threat, she happily showed him all around. He saw the stables and the lovely horses; there was one particular white horse who, the old woman explained, was so swift that he could overtake the wind and the wind behind him could not overtake him. Then she gave the *gosoon* a white rod and said that anything he would strike with the rod would immediately die.

She told him a story. 'There is a dragon who lives just off the coast there, and every year he would come in out of the sea to take a king's daughter off and devour her. Now, if the didn't get a king's daughter, the whole country would be destroyed by him.' With her guest continuing to listen eagerly, the woman continued. 'There came a man into the king's court and said that he would kill the dragon if the king gave him a year's supply of good food. The king readily agreed but so far the man has failed to kill the dragon.'

The next day the farmer's boy was going out to plough, as he was hired to do, and the farmer said to him, 'You need not be going out to plough today, *gosoon*, for everyone is going out to the sea to see the dragon taking away the king's daughter.'

'I will not be bothered going, Sir, for I have much work to be doing and will continue with the ploughing,' said the boy. When he was sure that the farmer was gone, he went back over the high wall, jumped on the back of the white horse and, with his white rod in his pocket, galloped down to the shore to challenge the dragon.

When he got to the sea he heard the bellowing roars of the dragon, and continued on out into the sea on his steed to face him. A great battle ensued, and with the great elements of fire and water clashing, hours of conflict passed between them. Suddenly the dragon became distracted and the *gosoon* took the opportunity and struck him with the rod, killing him stone dead.

There was great rejoicing on the shoreline when the boy rode back in on his white horse. The king's daughter thanked him and, taking a pair of golden scissors out of her pocket, cut a lock of hair from above his left ear and put it in a small golden box. Seeing that his duty was done, the *gosoon* rode away and returned the horse to the stable.

The following day, the king invited all the countryside to go to a feast in his castle and the man who told the king he would kill the dragon went along too. The king thought that this was the man who killed the dragon, and the man said nothing to the contrary.

Knowing that this was not right, the king's daughter took the box from her pocket and looked to see if there was any hair missing behind his ear, which there was not.

She went around and found the boy with the missing hair and said, 'This is my hero. This is the man who killed the dragon.'

The king set the record straight and gave his daughter in marriage to the *gosoon*, and every day they spent together from that day forward was happier than the one previous.

O'HANLON OF ULSTER

There was a fine young specimen of a man by name of O'Hanlon. Now, O'Hanlon had a strong constitution with the most amiable of countenances. Not only this, but his strength and prowess were unparalleled anywhere in the baronies of Ulster.

You'd be forgiven for thinking that such a young man would have all that was going for him, and you'd be right, but something turned. The fine lad began to dwindle and fade; his eyes dulled and his massive muscles shrank and shrivelled, and it was not long before he began to go off food altogether. After some time, he grew so weak that he was unable to rise from his bed, and although nobody could figure out for what ailed him, people began to think that the only place he was heading for was the grave.

The servants of the household continued to make his usual food, and even all his favourites, but letting out the most horrid groans and lamentations, he never touched a morsel.

His father, being greatly perturbed about the situation with his only son and heir, sent for three doctors to come and find out what sort of disease had struck down his once proud offspring, and he offered a big reward to the medic who could diagnose and treat the condition.

The three doctors arrived on the agreed day with their bags full of equipment. One by one, they spent hours with the young lad, poking and prodding him everywhere conceivable in an effort to stumble upon an answer, but they could put no name on the sickness nor think of a remedy to relieve it. They had to admit that they were stumped and they came down the stairs from the room and reluctantly reported that the affliction had them baffled entirely.

'Am I to lose my son, who is the finest boy in all of Ireland?' said the father. Now one of the doctors had a man with him, a quiet, very softly spoken person, and he upped and said, 'Maybe your honours would be giving me permission to visit the young gentleman. I have a tongue on me that is sweet and which draws the secrets of the world out of men, women, and children with great ease.'

Well, they brought him up to the room and left him alone with O'Hanlon. He sat down by the side of the bed and started out by flattering him with such conversation that was never heard before. After much small talk, he said, 'Let your Lordship's honour be telling me, what is it that ails you?'

Whilst making sure that the conversation would not go further than the two of them, O'Hanlon told the man, 'It is no disease on me, but the most terrible of misfortunes. It is in love I am.'

'Sure it is only the *grá* that you have. We've all been there, lad. It's nothing that should have you in this state,' said the man.

Still being confused at this, O'Hanlon went on to explain. 'The way of it is this; I am lamenting for a lady that does not walk the earth, nor for one who is dead that I could be following to the grave. I have a wee statue that has the most beautiful face on it that was ever seen, and it is destroyed with grief I am that it will never be speaking to me at all.'

With that, he took the statue out from under his pillow, and the loveliness of it made the man leap off the chair, but he said, 'Let me reassure you that that is the likeness of a lady who lives in the world at the present time and you will be finding her surely.' With that he went down below, where the three doctors and the old man were waiting and, despite the promise he made young O'Hanlon, he told the lot of them all he had heard.

The doctors allowed that if the gentleman's life was to be saved, he must be got out of his bed and sent away on his travels to find this woman, hoping that the travels themselves would divert him from his folly. So they all went up to the room and told young O'Hanlon to rise from his bed and eat a good dinner, for the grandest arrangements were made for his future and he'd surely meet the lady that had caused him so much grief. When O'Hanlon saw that no person was mocking him, he got into the best of humour, and he came down and reluctantly feasted with them. He then took the big handful of money he was offered and set out on his travels, taking the statue with him.

He went over the provinces of Ireland, then departed for England, then France, and, in fact visited every other part of the world in search of the lady who had stolen his heart, and in the process, his scruples. He had the strangest and most wonderful of adventures, and saw more wonders than could ever be told or remembered. At the latter end, he came back to the old country again, with no more than a coin or two left in his pocket.

The whole time he had never seen a lady who was the least like the wee statue he kept in his satchel. He knew by then that the words of the old doctor were only a cod, for he didn't quit thinking of her at all.

The hope was near dead in his heart and the sickness of grief was starting to creep up on him again when he came home to Ireland. Soon after he landed from the ship, he chanced to come on a gentleman's place and a fine big house it was too, the kind he never had seen before. He went up and enquired of the servants if he would get leave to rest there and received a most gracious reception.

The master of the house was very pleased to host such an agreeable guest and took heed at the concern expressed by his servants over the lack of food he was consuming. Thinking he had done something wrong, he said to O'Hanlon, 'Is the food in this place not to your liking, young *ladeen*?'

O'Hanlon assured him, 'There was never better refreshments set before an emperor.'

Knowing that something wasn't quite right with the young lad, the gentleman recommended an excellent doctor in the locality, but O'Hanlon said, 'Doctors have no relief for the sort of tribulation that is destroying me and I fear that the sickness on me will be the means of my death; I do not want to reward your kindness with the botheration of a corpse.'

He brought out the statue and showed it to the gentleman, explaining in detail and from start to finish the whole mighty mess he was in. With this, the gentleman's look of concern turned to a smile and he said, 'Fear not, young *ladeen*, for the lady that you seek is near this place on this very day. She goes down to the stream every day with six waiting maids in tow, and them bringing a rod and line for to fish.'

Well, I can tell you this right here and now, O'Hanlon was leaping wild with joy to hear tell of the lady.

'You will have your reward if you do strictly all I'm saying,' the gentleman advised. 'I'll provide you with the best of fishing tackle and you will go down to the stream to fish in it too. Whatever you catch on your line must be given to the lady as a gift when she passes but say nothing that might scare her off, and do not follow after her if she turns to go home.'

The next day O'Hanlon went out for to fish; not long was he at the stream before the lady came down with the six waiting maids following behind her. Sure enough she was the picture of the statue, and she had the loveliest golden hair that was ever to be seen in Ulster.

O'Hanlon had the luck to catch a noble trout and, taking it off the hook, he rolled it in leaves and took it to the lady, according to the advice of the gentleman. She was very pleased to accept the gift of the fish, but didn't she then turn home at once with the six waiting maids following along behind, as before. When she went into her own house, she took the fish to her father. 'There was a noble person at the stream this day and he made me a present of the trout,' she said.

Hoping to see her again, O'Hanlon returned the next day and, casting his line into the stream, he saw the lady coming along the bank and her six waiting maids walking behind her. Once again, he caught a splendid fine trout, bigger than the previous one, and after rolling it in leaves, he brought it over to her, but with that she turned around and headed home at once, just as the day before. The lady told her father of the new, bigger fish, and said that if the same happened again the next day that she would invite him back to partake in the refreshments of their place.

'Let you do as best pleases yourself,' said her father.

Well, sure as we are standing here, O'Hanlon got the biggest trout of all on the following day. The lady was in the height of humour, and she asked if he would go up to the house with her that day. She walked with O'Hanlon beside her and the six waiting maids following behind them.

They conversed very pleasantly together, and at last he found the courage to tell her of how he travelled the world to seek no person less than herself. 'I'm fearing you'll need to set out on a second journey,' said she. 'I have an old father who is after refusing two score of suitors and they asking for me off of him. I do be thinking I'll not get joining the world at all.'

She explained that her father had high expectations, and that 'unless a king would be persuading himself of the advancement there is in it for himself in having a son-in-law wearing a golden crown upon his head', he would not accept any suitors. She then said, 'The whole time it is great freedom I have, and I walk where it pleases me with six waiting maids along with me. The old man has a notion they would inform him if I was up to any diversion, but that is not the way of it at all.'

O'Hanlon, being confused, asked, 'If himself is that uneasy about you, how would it be possible you'd bring me to the house to be speaking with him?' She assured him that he was a reasonable man in all other matters, who received all his guests with great kindness,' but 'let you not be speaking of marriage with me, for he cannot endure to hear tell of the like.'

Well, the old man made O'Hanlon very welcome and he had no suspicion that the two were in notion of other. Their love for each other grew so fast and in such a short space, didn't they arrange and plan out an elopement all unbeknownst to the father?

O'Hanlon went back to the gentleman and told him all. 'But,' said he, 'I am after spending my whole great fortune of money travelling the territory of the world. I must be finding a good situation so I can make suitable provision for herself.' O'Hanlon then told the gentleman of the elopement and he gave them grand assistance, including a generous loan to start out on their life together.

They bought a lovely house and land with the money that was lent by the gentleman and after a wee while, O'Hanlon got a good commission to be an officer; nothing more in the world was needful to their happiness. Both he and his lady had a fine life. They lacked for no comfort nor splendour at all. O'Hanlon saved up what money was left over to repay the loan to the gentleman only for a few pounds.

The officer's commission he had been given brought him over to England from time to time, and the lady O'Hanlon would mind the household until he was home. One evening in merry old England, O'Hanlon was having a few wee drams with a fellow officer in the mess. Now, this officer was a droll sort of a man and not the best of influences.

O'Hanlon was boasting about his fine wife at home, and the Englishman, wanting to get a rise out of him for a bit of entertainment, said, 'Don't you know, rightly when you are not in the house that herself will be feasting and entertaining and going on with every diversion?' Now, I can tell you here and now, that this was a great insult and that O'Hanlon was hopping mad at the impertinence of the suggestion.

The Englishman, in all his conniving arrogance, offered O'Hanlon a bet. 'Let you make a powerful big bet with myself that I will not be able to bring you a token from your lady and a full description of her appearance.' Knowing how faithful his lady was, O'Hanlon gladly took the bet, saying, 'I'll surely be taking that money off you. 'Tis only a fool's bet you have made.'

'I'm not in the least uneasy about it, for I'm full sure it's the truth I'm after speaking of how she does be playing herself in your absence.'

The Englishman took the ship to Ireland, and he came to the house of the lady O'Hanlon, where she was in the kitchen making a cake. On seeing the man walking up to the door, she stopped what she was doing and away she ran to the parlour, but in the hurry forgot the lovely pearl ring she took off her finger when she began at the baking. Well, on seeing the door standing open, he let himself in and saw the unattended ring on the kitchen table. It was easy knowing that this was no common article and that this could not be in the possession of anyone but the mistress of the house. What did the lad do? But, he only went and slipped it into his pocket, the pup.

The Lady O'Hanlon sent her waiting maid down to enquire as to his business with them, and he just said that he was a weary traveller looking for to rest somewhere. He began for to flatter the girl and to offer her bribes, and in the latter end he got her to speak. She told him all what the mistress of the house was like; how she had a mole under her right arm and one on her left knee.

Moreover she gave him a few long golden hairs she got out of the lady's comb.

The Englishman went back to O'Hanlon, bringing with himself the tokens, and demanding immediate payment of the bet. Thinking that his lady had betrayed him, O'Hanlon had to pay the bet using the money he had saved up to pay back the gentleman.

O'Hanlon sent word to his wife that he was coming home and asked for her to meet him on the ship. She put her finest attire and started away at once, very much looking forward to be reunited with her love, but when she arrived at the dock and stepped aboard the ship, she realised that not all was well.

She went up on the deck where she had seen her husband standing, and on seeing her he turned around and looked the other way. When she went over to speak with him, he would not answer. When she reached out to embrace him, he pushed her away in a fit of jealous rage and she suddenly fell into the water. Then he went on shore, full sure she had drowned. But there was another ship coming in, and a miller that was on board had seen the lady struggling in the sea. He was an aged man, yet he knew right from wrong, and so he ventured in after her and he saved the poor creature's life.

Well, the miller was a good sort of a man and he had great compassion for herself when she told him her story. She had no knowledge of the cause of her husband being vexed with her, and she thought it hard to believe the evidence of her senses that he was after striving to make away with her. The miller advised the lady O'Hanlon to remain on the ship until they reached the next port, for if she returned home on this night, O'Hanlon may try to finish the job of doing away with her.

When the ship came into harbour, the news was going of a great lawsuit. The miller heard all, and he brought word to the lady that O'Hanlon was in danger of being put to death. 'There are three charges against him,' said the miller. 'The first being his impeachment for stealing you away and you not being wishful to be with him; the second for his failure to repay a debt to a gentleman; and the third, and most grievous, for his murder of yourself.'

Said she, 'These are all false charges. Firstly, I was not stolen against my will, for I helped to plan the whole elopement. Secondly, the money was all gathered up for to pay the debt, and thirdly, seeing as you saved me in that ill hour, I am not dead.' Whatever madness has come over him, my feelings for him remain true. I had better be giving evidence in the court of law, or it will be the gallows for my love.'

The lady and the miller turned around and returned to the original docks where she had been flung into the sea, and went as quickly as they could to the courthouse where O'Hanlon was being tried. When they got there, the sentence had just been passed, and he was sentenced to hang by the neck. With that the Lady O'Hanlon stood up in the court and gave out that she had not been put to death at all.

They began the whole trial over again and, degree by degree, the various truths came to light, as they invariably do. The villainy and deceit of the Englishman were uncovered and it was decreed that the money was to be restored by him, and the gentleman was to get his payment out of it.

The Lady O'Hanlon's father was in such ecstasy at seeing his daughter, and she alive, that he forgave her and the husband for the elopement. Sure, the three of them went away home together and they were the happiest people were ever heard tell of in the world.

WAKING KATIE

Katie was married to Pat, but she lived by herself, seeing as he was employed in overseas lands. Poor Katie, God be good to her, was a strange kind of a soul; pale and scared looking, with one blue eye in her head and the other one grey.

Something ailed her, the poor *craythur*, and she had some kind of a thing that came over her from time to time, which caused her a great fluttering in her heart. Sometimes she would be struck down by it for a couple of hours, and all the while she was afflicted she'd be thinking she was drowning.

Many of the neighbours thought that she was 'not all there'. They could not put their finger on it, but they knew that there was something amiss.

So crippled was she by what ailed her that she said, 'No person can give me the least relief in the world, of which I am not long for. I'll be making but one request of my friends and neighbours, and that be that there be no whiskey at the wake.'

'Sure the like was never heard tell of before,' said the woman of the house, '… and what use would there be in a wake as dry as a stick?'

'Maybe no use in at all, as you are after saying,' answered Katie, 'but let you pay heed to my words or there's likely to be a queer story told at the end of time.' Said the woman of the house, 'Surely you'll be a beautiful corpse and every one of us paying our best respects to you all the same.'

Not a long time after this, wasn't poor Katie found in her own house and she sprawled dead on the floor of the kitchen.

All the friends and neighbours gathered in for the wake, and what had they along with them? Only a beautiful jar of the finest whiskey. They could not think to give in to the arrangement herself set out, that they'd remain in the place with a parching drought for company. The whole party was sitting round and singing a wee song, and all the while the jar of itself was in the middle of the floor. There came a loud noise and shouting on the street, as if there was a powerful assembly of people and then there was a great battering on the windows. The door suddenly swung wide open with a large crack and the disturbance came into the kitchen, yet no person sitting there could see anything causing the unearthly commotion. It was a rightly queer gathering surely, for the friends and neighbours of the dead were silent and still, and the crying went round them on the air.

After a while the jar of whiskey let a leap out of it and began to roll on the floor. It was turned again and every drop teemed from it before the watching eyes. The disturbance then passed from the kitchen, and away down the field; whatever was last to go closed the door behind all.

A man stood up and he said, 'This is no right gathering surely, and we would do well to be gone.' With that, another door flew open and all present made themselves ready to depart without any delay, but on looking out the door they could hear fiddles, pipes, and laughter. This was no ordinary joviality but the kind of merriment that was not of this earth. The fear grew quickly in them and the anxiety to quit the house slowed to a halt.

They cowered in beside the hearth, knowing that they had paid no heed to the deceased's last wishes. 'Sure isn't the ruckus down there beyond from the Fear Dubh (devil) himself, and he having the wake without us and with our whiskey,' said a man.

Another man urged his brother, 'Let us come on away home, for what enticement is on us to stay when the drink is gone from us to the dark fella down there.' Thinking the man pure crazy and frozen with fear, his brother would not budge from the house and neither would the others. They bid him well for his trip home by his lonesome in the darkness. Now this fella was a bold sort of a man, and it's likely he'd not have gone only for the reaction of the others in the house – he liked to be seen as the daring and brave kind, but the people thought anything but.

'You'll be snatched and devoured by the Fear Dubh, and he in great humour after whipping off with the whiskey before our eyes.'

Sure enough, the man left the house and walked down by the end of the field; a horrific cry was heard and the man was not seen again. It is believed to this day that Katie herself was dining with the Fear Dubh at her own wake, and that it was horrid wonderful that she knew what might be taking place on the night of her departure from home.

JOHNNY AND THE MOON

Long ago there lived a man named Johnny, and his humble abode was that of a wee labourer's cottage on the local lord's estate. Johnny was a kind soul but, like most of us from time to time, was fairly lonely. He thought to himself that he should put this situation right as it was a poor thing to be living alone, so he went to his local matchmaker and came home with a wife.

I neglected to say earlier that Johnny had a bit of a vice in the form of his fondness for the drink.

One fine, frosty night, Johnny went into the estate office to draw his pay, and after doing so, headed for home when he met some neighbours on the road on their way into town. They said to him, 'Johnny, where are you going to on this bitter night?'

'I am going home,' said Johnny.

'Mick Dolan is playing the cards for to win a goose, and we want to give him a throw.' They persuaded Johnny to come along, with his pockets full of the week's wages. He went back with the neighbours, played for the goose, and had a few wee drams, but he was not the lucky one. They all played on until it was late in the night and then they started for home.

Remembering that he had promised his wife Molly not to be home too late, Johnny took a short cut through the bog. He crossed through hedges and over ditches and came to the middle of a bog. There he saw a flat stone, where he sat down to rest and have a smoke. He was not long sitting when a big gander flew down beside him. He wondered at the gander coming so near him. 'Good night, Johnny,' said the gander.

'I never thought geese could talk,' said Johnny.

'Oh, didn't you often hear us gabbing together?' said the gander. 'What do you want me to do?' asked Johnny.

'That goose that was played for in that house tonight was with me all harvest until the wild geese went up and she fell and left me.'

Telling the gander that he did not win the goose at the card game, he asked, 'What can I do?'

The gander replied, 'She will be played in another house and I need you to go again and win her so that she can be free.'

'I will do this', said Johnny, 'but now I must be going home.' The gander began to grow until he was as big as a horse and when Johnny got up on his back, he then flew up into the clouds and Johnny said, 'I know my way home and as sure as I'm sitting here, you are not flying me home.'

'Get off if you like, but you are better to stay where you are,' the gander responded.

He flew and flew until they both arrived on the moon. Johnny began to shout in anger, when the man in the moon opened the door and looked out, saying, 'What's all this shouting about?'

'Ah! Let me in!' said Johnny, 'let me in.'

The man in the moon replied, 'It is at home you ought to be this time of night.'

'Ah! I'm famished and in need of a dram, let me in!' shouted Johnny.

'I have no time! I have no time! I have to stoke the moon before she quenches.'

Johnny told the gander to take him home, and he obliged, but left him at the long flat stone where he picked him up. Johnny then thought of Molly and started for home, and when he reached the house he peeped in at the window and saw poor Molly sitting at the fire. He knocked on the window and she took a good grip at the tongs, asking, 'Who's here at this time of night?'

'I was up at the moon, Molly,' said he.

'Well, you can go straight back to the moon,' said she.

'I can't, Molly, my dear, the white gander is away.'

'God bless us and save us,' said she, 'poor Johnny must be out of his mind,' and with that she let him into the house, asking, 'What ails you Johnny?' She made him sit at the fire and made him a wee sup of tea and put him to bed. Molly then ran to a neighbour's house and the man there said that Johnny had one too many drams and had dreamed it all. 'Go home, put himself to his *leaba*, and do the same to yourself,' said he.

From that day to this, Johnny believes he was at the moon.

MICK McAHEANEY'S MISFORTUNE

In a remote place on a backward part of the mountain lived Mick McAheaney. It was the same place where Mick had been born and raised, and it was said that he entered the world at midnight on Friday 13th, and the cock that was in the barn crowed thirteen times. It was also rumoured that the hens began to fly up and down throughout the barn with fright and one of the hens was so fretful that it managed to escape out under the door and shook her feathers, crowing thirteen times. A strange occurrence, you must agree.

Now, normally the birth of a child is a joyous occasion for a family, but not this one. Something terrible crept over the household. A kind of unspeakable fear.

So great was the anxiety of the nurse who was minding his mother that she continually asked Mick's father to go out and twist the head off the cock who was crowing so much and throw it over the roof of the house. Finally he agreed to do this, and so went out to the barn, but on reaching the door he found himself surrounded by fairies, and them none too happy.

They took him captive but he succeeded in obtaining his release by turning his coat inside out and slipping out through the quickset hedge. He made for home as quickly as he could but on seeing the light from the house, fell and sprained his ankle. He was to be lame from that day until the time of his natural death.

He said, 'Weren't the wee people only on their way to carry the young lad off with themselves. They're fierce unhappy to hear the warning crows of a cock in the night, and much less that of a hen.'

Poor Mick grew up a very sickly, delicate boy and it is believed that the *mí-ádh* was left on him by the fairies.

THE CHARM

There was once an old woman who was always seen wandering here and wandering there. She had nothing to live on and had to go around looking for charity from people.

One day she knocked on the door of a well-to-do man, asking for some charity. Not wanting to be seen as rude by anybody, the man let her in. The woman did, however, irk him somewhat as she was always coming to him, and he knew that this wasn't the first time and likely not the last. In an effort to put her off, he said to her, 'I will give you a charm, young lady, that you might make a living on it. When you hear of anybody being sick, say the charm.' He went on to explain that it should be said in this way: 'I'll rub you up and I'll rub you down, and if I'll do you no good, I'll do you no harm.'

So the old lady went on her way and thanked him. From that day on, she took it upon herself to visit everybody in the townland who was sick and say the charm to them. Strange to say, they used to get better and would give her plenty of money.

Many years later, the man who had given her the charm got very sick and all good doctors in the land were unable to cure him, so they were resigned to give him up for death. The old woman came into the house where he was and his wife was huddled over her husband in the bed and crying over his fate. The woman asked the wife what the matter with her was and she told the woman that her husband was dying with a lump in his throat.

The woman said the charm for him and when the man heard her saying the words, he could not contain his laughter. It was with the laugh that the lump burst and he was cured.

St Brigid's Head

In Ireland, the season of spring is still traditionally celebrated on 1 February. This day is also the feast of St Brigid in the new calendar and the Goddess Brigid in the old.

Brigid, in all her guises, was – and continues to be – widely venerated throughout Cavan and all of Ireland. When Christianity originally arrived in Cavan, the Goddess was widely revered among the natives and to protect their idol, they hid a carved sandstone

head representing her for safekeeping in one of the ancient mounds that dot this landscape.

We can only assume that one of the disciples of St Mogue or St Feidhlim was so convincing that the locals gave up their idol, who was then housed in newly built local church of Knockbride, where she became known as St Bride.

During the time of the Famine, when the poor Irish were busy trying not to starve to death, a parish priest of the area, Father Owen O'Reilly, had a new church built. Whilst he was transporting the idol of Brigid from the old church to the new in his donkey cart, he noticed that it was emitting a certain hum and vibration in the back of his cart. When he began to pass Rooskey Lough, suddenly the head gave a strange screech, jumped up off the cart and leaped into the murky depths of the lough, where it is assumed that it remains to this day.

BRIDE OF THE DEVIL

There once was a strong farmer, and he was a proud and boastful man. He lived in a well-proportioned, comfortable place and sure enough, to hear him speaking you'd be thinking his house was built of solid silver and thatched with the purest of gold thread.

Herself was a very different *craythur* altogether; kind, gentle, and generous. She took no pleasure in making out that she was something that she was not, and unlike her husband, she was not envious, greedy, or uncharitable.

The two had but one child, a fine daughter who was their main delight in the whole world. Bríde was a beautiful girl, with the finest of countenances that would charm a king from his golden throne to be walking the bogs with her. The boys flocked after her by the score, and she had but to raise her hand to draw any one of them to her side.

Being a seemly, well-reared lass, she took her diversion without any consideration of marriage at all; she was well satisfied that her father would make a fitting settlement for her when the time came. The youth of the world will always be playing and chatting together, all the while them that have right wit and a good upbringing do leave their settlement in the hands of the parents have the best understanding for the same. This will horrify many to hear, but that was the way of things back in the day.

'I'm thinking,' said himself one evening, 'that it's old and stiff I am growing. It might be a powerful advantage to take a son-in-law into the place, that way I'd get sitting in peace by the hearth, and he out in the fields attending to the management of it all.'

'Bríde is too young to be joining the world,' said his wife. 'But I will not be putting any hindrance in the way of it, for maybe it's better contented she'd be to have a fine man of her own instead of looking on an old pair like ourselves, and we dozing by the fire of an evening.'

'I'll need to be building them a wee settlement for to raise a brood, surely,' said he to himself.

The next day he announced throughout the country that Bríde was to be married and what with a little handful of money, the fine farm of land, and the looks of the girl, the suitors were coming in aplenty. Suitors came in all shapes and sizes. From big strong farmers to small farmers, from tradesmen to dealers and blacksmiths, from vets to travelling salesmen. The farmer was disgusted with all of them, and put them all out in a very civil but stiff manner.

In next strolled a good-looking young lad by the name of Alec. He was known as a hard worker and had a wee bit of money behind him that was left him by his own Da. 'Now if you were to seek all

Ireland ten times through, I'll go bail you wouldn't be finding a more suitable match than Alec and Bríde,' said the farmer's wife to her husband. The girl and her mother were fair wild with delight, but they got an odious disappointment, for didn't he run the poor boy out of the house. 'I'm fierce surprised at you,' said the wife. 'Pray tell, why couldn't you have wit and give that decent lad an honourable reception? A better match for her like isn't walking this earth.'.

'I'd sooner let the Devil have her than see her join the world with that Alec. I'll have you know,' said he, 'that I'll have a gentleman for my son-in-law and no common person at all.'

'It is the raving of prosperity that is on you,' said she. 'And that is the worst madness of it all.'

Not long afterwards, a splendid gentleman came to the house, riding on a horse. 'I have heard tell,' said he to the farmer, 'that you are seeking a suitable settlement for your daughter.'

'If your honour wants a wife,' said the farmer, 'let you be stepping in, for it is maybe in this house you'll find her.'

With that the gentleman got down off his horse, and it was an honourable reception they made him. Even the wife was content to remember the scorn put on poor Alec now she had seen the magnificent suitor who had come. The gentleman had a smile on his face when he heard all the boasts of the farmer. 'My good man', said he, 'I think scorn on your money and land, for I'd have you to know that I am a king in my own place. But that girl sitting by the hearth has a lovely countenance on her, and her heart I am seeking for love of the same'.

'Oh mother, will you send him away?' moaned Bríde. 'I'd go through fire and water for my poor Alec!'

'Will you hold your whisht,' replied her mother. 'That is no right talk for a well-reared girl.'

The farmer and the gentleman made their agreement and opened the bottle of whiskey. There was to be a nice little feast to celebrate the settlement, and the cloth was set in the parlour on account of the grandeur of the suitor and him not being used to a kitchen at all. When the supper was served, didn't the servant girl call the mistress out to the kitchen.

'Oh ma'am', says she. 'I couldn't get word with you in private before. Let you hunt that lad from the place.'

The wife responded, 'And why, might I ask?'

'Sure how would he be a right gentleman and he having a foot on him like a goat?' said the girl.

With that, the mistress began to lament and to groan. 'What'll I do? What'll I do? I'm scared useless with dread'

'I'll go in and impeach him,' said the servant girl, and, right enough, in she went to the parlour. 'Quit off out of this,' said she. 'We'll have no goat feet in this place!'

The farmer was that set in his own conceit that he just answered, 'What harm is in a reel foot? It's no ornament surely, but that's all there is to it.'

'Many's the reel foot I've laid eyes on,' she says. 'But yon is the hoof of a goat.'

'Aye, it is truth you are speaking,' said the gentleman. 'I am the Devil and no person less. But you can't put me out, for the man of the house has me promised to his daughter.'

'There is no person living might have power on the soul of another. If my sins don't deliver me into your hand, the word of my Da is no use,' said Bríde. 'Then I'll be taking himself,' declared the Devil, making ready to go.

'You may wait till he's dead,' cried the woman of the house. 'He made you no offer of his bones and his flesh.'

'The tongues of three women would argue the Devil to death,' said he, and away he went in a grey puff of smoke.

The man and woman of the house knelt down for to pray. But said the farmer to the servant, 'Let you slip off to Alec and bid him to come up, for it is an honourable reception he will now get at this place.'

GETTING THE HUMP

There was once a peculiar man named Jack who lived on Church Lane in the town of Cavan. Poor auld Jack was struck down with an affliction whereby he could only look down at the ground. His sight was no better than a blind man's for all the use it was to him as he could not look up to see where he was going. The reason for this was because of a big fatty hump that grew out of the back of his neck. He was always followed around and mocked by the children of the town and it made Jack fierce unhappy.

Now, Jack had one bit of enjoyment in his life and that was in his penchant for being a bit of a gossip-monger. He loved a bit of news and could not be trusted to stay quiet with any bit of a secret that came his way. This habit got him into more than one bit of trouble over the years.

One day, when Jack was having a pint in the town, he got chatting to a man visiting from the country. 'I shouldn't be saying this,' said he, 'but sure isn't there an old biddy out by Swellan who can put the cure of it on your hump?' Jack was fascinated to hear more and so the man told him more. 'Didn't I have a big hump meself not so long ago, and look at me back now. Straight as a pin, so it is.' Jack bought the man a whiskey with excitement and headed straight out to the biddy at Swellan to obtain the cure.

He came to the cottage and knocked on the door. 'I hear you're the biddy who can rid me of my hump,' said he to she.

'I am,' said the biddy. 'I can do it for a piece of silver and the promise that you tell nobody.' Jack duly agreed and handed her over two and six. With that, the biddy took out a twig of hawthorn and said some kind of a prayer under her breath before gently tapping it on his hump. He went back home and went to bed, somewhat disappointed with the hump still on his back.

The next morning, Jack arose spritely like never before and jumped out of bed, knowing something was different! Different in a good way – his hump was gone! He ran outside and took the old dusty bicycle from the shed. He had not ridden it for years, but on this occasion jumped on it and cycled in through the town, looking at everything all around him. Everybody stopped to look at the new Jack, with his back as straight as a pin.

He jumped off the bike outside the pub and ran in. On seeing the countryman sitting at the bar, he ordered two whiskies and thanked him for his advice. Something did not look right to Jack. The countryman looked sad and kept his eyes on the floor. 'What's the matter?' said Jack. 'Sure isn't it a glorious day!' The countryman drank up and left in a hurry, saying, 'Just keep your promise!' on the way out. Jack was confused what he meant by this but noticed to his horror that the countryman had a massive hump on his neck when only yesterday he had none.

Jack ordered a few more pints and was enjoying the comfortable surroundings of the tavern when a young lad walked in on crutches. 'Sure, sit down here, *ladeen*, and I'll buy ye a drink. I'm celebrating,' said Jack. Jack saw that the *ladeen* also had a hump, and began to feel sorry for him, as he could see a younger him in the *ladeen*. 'I shouldn't be saying this,' said he, 'but sure isn't there an old biddy out by Swellan who can put the cure of it on your hump.' In no time at all, the *ladeen* was gone and Jack went home to sleep off the drink.

The next day Jack awoke with his bones creaking and his neck aching. He got out of bed and found himself only able to look at the

floor. 'Aaaagh!' he screamed. 'Me hump is back!' The sadness of the world fell back upon him and he decided to go for another drink when he saw the *ladeen* in the bar, all happy and sprightly. Only then did he realise what had happened. Jack got up and left, saying on the way out, 'Just keep your promise!'

The King of France's Daughter

The bones of this particular tale have come from the excellent 1912 publication of *Folk Tales of Breffny* by B. Hunt.

There was once an old man who was terribly poor, and he lived by his lonesome in a small wee shack by the roadside. In the mornings he would go out to gather sticks in a nearby wood; this way he'd have a bright fire to be sitting at of an evening. One bitter cold night that the old man heard a rapping at the door. He went over and when he opened it, he saw a poor little boy in a red cap standing outside; frozen to the bone he was, the poor creature. 'Let you come in straight away and warm yourself at the fire,' said he, for he always had a good reception for every person.

The wee *ladeen* with the red cap walked in and stopped for a good while, conversing with the old man whilst he regained the feeling in his frozen limbs. He was the best of company, and the old man didn't find the time passing until the *ladeen* rose for to go. 'Let you come in and rest yourself here any evening you are out in these parts, for I'll not have any friend of mine wandering around in weather such as this,' said the kind old gent.

The very next night the little fellow was in it again, and the night after that, warming himself at the warm, bright fire and talking away. Said he, 'I do be thinking it is bitter poor you are!'

'That I surely am, no doubt about it,' said the old man.

'Well, let you pay attention to me – it is the truth I'm speaking – you'll have more gold than ever you'll contrive for to spend,' said the *ladeen*. 'I am determined to make a rich man of you for all the kindness you have shown me.' The *ladeen* went on, 'You see, there is a lady at the point of death, and she is the King of France's daughter. I have a bottle here in my pocket, and that is the cure for the disease is on her. I'll be giving it to you, and let you set out for France at the morning of the day. When you come to the

King's palace the servants will bid you be gone for an ignorant beggar, but let you not be heeding them at all. Don't quit asking to see the king, and in the latter end they'll give in to you. It is with himself the most difficulty will be, for that man will think it hard to believe the likes of a poor old Irishman could have a better cure nor all the doctors in the world. A power of them allowed they'd have her right well in no time, and but it was worse they left her. The king is giving out that the next person coming with a false cure will lose their life. Let you not be scared at that decree, for you are the man that shall succeed. You may promise to have the lady fit to ride out hunting in nine days. Three drops from the bottle is all you have to give her, and that for three mornings after other.'

The old man paid great heed to all the *ladeen* in the red cap was telling him. He took the wee bottle that was to make him a rich man, and he made ready to set out at the morning of the day. He was a long time travelling the world before he came to the palace where the King of France's daughter was lying at the point of death. The servants mocked the poor old Irishman, but he paid no attention to their words at all. In the latter end he got to see the king, and that gentleman allowed the likes of this gent could never succeed when the doctors of the world were failing.

'I will only be having the head cut off you, monsieur!' said the king.

'I'm not the least bit in dread, your honour,' said the old man. 'The lady is bound to be ready to ride out hunting in nine days, if she uses my medicine.' His perseverance and courage won over the King of France, and permission was given for a trial of the cure.

The first morning, after taking the three drops from the bottle, the lady turned in her bed. The second morning, after the treatment, she sat up and ate her food. The third morning, when she had taken the three drops, the King of France's daughter rose from her bed. And in nine days she was ready to ride out hunting, just as the young *ladeen* said.

They could not do enough for him; there was great gratitude in them. Well, the reward he accepted was a big sack of gold, and that was the load he brought home to his cabin in Ireland.

The first evening he was sitting by his clear fire, the little boy came in at the door. 'Didn't I do well for you?' says he.

'Aye, you did surely, *ladeen*. I have more gold in that sack than ever I'll contrive to spend.'

'Will you be doing me a service in return for all?' said the *ladeen*.

'Indeed and I will,' said himself.

'We have all arranged to cross over to France this night and wish to bring away the lady you cured, the king's daughter of that country,' said the *ladeen*. 'But we cannot contrive to accomplish the like unless we have flesh and blood along with us. Will you come?'

The old man duly agreed and with that they went out the door and across the road into the field. It was thronged with regiments of the good people, past belief or counting. They were running every way through the field, calling out, 'Get me a horse, get me a horse!' And what were they doing only cutting down the *sceachs* and riding away on them. 'Get me a horse, get me a horse!' said himself, calling out along with them.

But the fellow in the red cap came over to him looking terrible vexed. 'Don't let another word out of you,' says he. 'Except one of ourselves speaks first. Mind what I'm telling you or it will be a cause of misfortune.'

'I'll say no more except in answer to a question,' said the old man.

With that they brought him a white yearling calf, and put him up to ride upon it. He thought it was a queer sort of a horse, but he passed no remarks. And away they rode at a great pace, the good people on the *sceachs* and the old man on the yearling calf.

They made grand going, and it wasn't long before they came to a big lake that had an island in the middle of it. With one spring, the whole party landed on the island and with another, they were safe on the far shore. 'Damn, but that was a great lep for a yearling calf,' says the old man. With that one of the good people struck him a blow on the head, the way the sense was knocked out of him and he fell on the field.

At daylight the old man came to himself, and he lying on the field by the big lake. He was a long journey from home, and he was weary travelling round the water and over the hills to his own place. But the worst of all was the sacks of gold: didn't every bit of the fortune melt away and leave him poor, the way he was before he came in with the good people.

WILL O' THE WISP AND THE MAN FROM DOWNSTAIRS

There once lived a blacksmith named Jack, and he, being a very bad man, never did a good deed for anybody. He snarled at everybody who went by and would never spend a shilling on anything. So mean was he that the locals took to calling him 'Stingy Jack'! He never gave a single sinner a decent greeting. He even lost all his childhood friends because of his mean-spirited ways.

Stingy Jack would pass his time sitting over one pint all day in the bar and reading newspapers that others had left. The landlord in the pub was growing impatient with Stingy Jack, seeing as he had not paid anything off his tab in a long time and it was growing to be sizeable. Said he to the landlord, 'Sure, amen't I good for it?' but he knew that he was not.

So bad was Stingy Jack's temperament that nobody would come near him to give him any work, choosing instead to go to the blacksmith in the next village over. It was not long before Stingy Jack became very poor and the landlord would not let him back into the bar until he settled his tab.

One day, Stingy Jack was walking along the road with a fierce rumbling in his stomach and a mighty thirst on his lips, when a man appeared alongside him. 'I am the man from downstairs,' said he. 'I will give you one wish if you come to me in twenty years.' Knowing that this was the Devil himself, Jack agreed. 'Pay my bar tab and I will come to you in twenty years,' said Jack. The Devil agreed, they shook hands, and off they went on their way.

Stingy Jack continued to lead as awful a life as he had done before meeting the 'man from downstairs' and in no time twenty years had passed. He saw the Devil coming up the road when he climbed a tree in his garden. 'Climb this tree and I will come to hell with you,' said Jack, so the Devil climbed the tree and just before he was able to grab him, Jack jumped down quickly and carved a cross with his penknife in the trunk of the tree. The Devil was stuck up the tree and could not climb down, as he was unable to pass the cross that Jack had carved. 'We had an agreement! You have tricked the ultimate *sleveen*!' yelled the Devil.

'I will let you down if you release me from my due,' said Jack. Reluctantly, the Devil had no option but to agree and, scratching the cross off the bark, Jack let him come down.

Another twenty years passed and Jack had still never mended his mean-spirited ways. It was now that he was on his deathbed and slowly passed over. When he finally died, he ascended to the gates of Heaven and spoke with St Peter. 'I am very sorry, Jack,' said St Peter, 'but I cannot let you into Heaven because of the wicked life you have led.' Knowing this to be true, Jack was unable to argue

with St Peter. With this, a trap door opened in the cloud he was standing on and he tumbled down to the gates of Hell.

The Devil came to the gates and said, 'Hello Stingy Jack, nice of you to visit!'

'Visit?' asked Jack, 'I am here to stay. Make up my room!'

'You'll not be staying here. You are too much of a *sleveen*, even for me,' said the Devil, and handed him a lantern containing a single hot coal from the fires of the condemned.

With that, Jack was banished back to earth and forced to walk the bogs and moors with only a single coal to light his way. He soon withered away to a wisp and passed his time in tricking weary travellers and leading them astray with the light from his lantern. He was to be forever known as Will o' the Wisp.

The Man with Big Feet

One day a boy had become a man and needed a pair of man's shoes, but his feet had grown so big overnight that he could get no shoes to fit them. He made up his mind to go to Belfast and to try and get some shoes to fit him there.

He left the house and went on his way to Belfast but got lost along the way. Not knowing what to do, he walked on and on, but he could see nothing except a small house in the distance. On arriving at the house, he went over to it and knocked at the door; an old woman came out and told the man to come inside. He did so and on entering, saw two other old women sitting in front of the fire. One of the women gave him food, and she told him that he could stay all night if he so wished. When he had eaten his meal, the woman gave him a pair of shoes that fitted him. The man then went to bed and he pretended that he was asleep. The three old women got up and each in turn opened the door, put on a cap, and said, 'High for over!' On hearing this, he thought he'd give it a go too, and so he got up and, seeing another cap left on the hook, he put it on his head and said, 'High for over!'

The next thing the *ladeen* knew was that he had landed with the three old women in a big store. Here he ordered drink, and when he had it drunk he had no money to pay for it. The police were sent for and the man was sentenced to death. He was to be hanged the next day according to the law of that land. When he was ready to be hanged, an old woman came crying. She said that she wanted to speak to the man that was going to be hanged.

When the woman got up to speak to him, she handed him a cap and told him to put it on him and say 'High for over!' This he did, and they both flew back to the cottage.

THE SHEAF OF WHEAT

There was once a very bad man named Kiernan who lived in the county. So bad was Kiernan that none of his neighbours liked him and nobody wanted to have anything to do with him. He was so wrapped up was in his own importance that this did not bother him one bit.

There also lived nearby a sweet angel of a girl called Caitlín, and in her was a good and kind heart. She was known by all for helping the poor and destitute and, despite her lacking of any wealth, she was said never to turn anybody away from her door who needed help. Caitlín lived with her father, who was very ill and was sure to die if he could not obtain the intervention of a doctor. Sadly, they had no money to pay for such a procedure.

Kiernan got to thinking that he should start to settle down and take a wife to look after him, and on hearing of Caitlín's plight, thought that he would turn this situation to his own advantage.

He went to see Caitlín and said that he would pay for her father's operation in return for her hand in marriage. 'I will agree, Mr Kiernan, if my father agrees,' Caitlín replied. Kiernan went to talk to the old man, and, knowing that he would die without the operation, he reluctantly agreed to Kiernan's proposal. They were married late the following week.

Kiernan took Caitlín to live with him, and it was not long before his true colours shone through. He forbade her to ever give food or shelter to anybody who came seeking it to the house. This was at a time when wives were expected to blindly obey their husbands, and so Caitlín told him she would do as he ordered.

It was some time after this, on a dark and stormy night, that Kiernan was drinking down in the local pub. On this night two holy men called to the door, begging, 'If it would please your ma'am, would you have some shelter for the night for us?' Poor Caitlín was conflicted, but knew that to give the men shelter on such a dreadful night was the right thing to do. She took the lantern and showed them the empty byre where they could sleep for the night, she then returned with a small slice of bread and milk for them to settle their stomachs.

It was not until later that evening that Kiernan returned from the pub and discovered the two holy men in the byre. Incensed with rage, he grabbed his shotgun and announced that they would be shot. 'Dear sir, grant us but one favour before we are sent to our maker,' said one of the men.

'What is that?' replied Kiernan.

'Allow me to preach one last sermon before we leave this earth.' With a wicked laugh, Kiernan agreed to this request as it would not cost him anything.

The holy man began to preach and so eloquent and passionate were his words that Kiernan felt his heart being touched by them. He was filled with remorse and started to beg the men's forgiveness.

He then searched round until he found some wheat. He took a bundle of this in his arms and made a bed for them whilst the tears of repentance coursed down his cheeks.

During the night one of the friars, in a dream, saw the Devil and Michael the Archangel with a pair of scales between them, on which they were weighing up the good and bad deeds of Kiernan. Just then, as the scales weighed heavily in favour of the Devil, St Michael took up a sheaf of wheat from the bed and threw it on the scales, meaning that it was suddenly weighed down on the good side, and of course Michael then claimed him for Heaven.

A few minutes afterwards, the men were awakened by a loud scream. It was Caitlín, the young woman who had given them the shelter in the first place. They ran in to see her weeping and wailing after discovering that her husband had passed away in his sleep during the night. The two men told her of their vision and not to worry about Kiernan for he was now in Heaven and that it was a sheaf of wheat that had won him his place there.

7

Wisdom

Riddles

Who doesn't like a good riddle now and again? Being masters of language, the Irish love a good brainteaser and tongue twister. Below are a few of my local favourites:

1.   What walks with its head down?
     A nails in your boot.

2.   When can water be eaten?
     When it is frozen.

3.   *What is the difference between a school master and a post office clerk?*
     One licks with a stick and another sticks with a lick.

4.   What goes up when the rain comes down?
     An umbrella.

5.   What is the difference between an engine driver and a school master?
     One minds the train and the other trains the minds.

6. What is the difference between a hill and a fill?
   One is hard to go up and the other hard to get down.

7. What turns without moving?
   Sour milk.

8. What is black and white and red all over?
   A newspaper.

9. What goes around and around the wood but never get into the wood?
   The bark of a tree.

10. Why is Ireland so like a bottle?
    Because it has a cork in it.

11. The man that made it never wore it, and the man that wore it never saw it. What is it?
    A coffin.

12. What is the difference between an aeroplane and a tree?
    One sheds leaves and the other leaves sheds.

13. Why is an elephant always ready for his holidays?
    Because he always has his trunk with him.

14. How many sides are there to a bucket?
    Two, inside and outside.

15. As I went out a slippery gap I met my uncle Davy. I cut off his head and I felt his body. What am I?
    A head of cabbage.

16.   What kind of tables do we eat?
       Vegetables.

SEANFHOCAIL – WISE OLD IRISH SAYINGS

The Irish have a wealth of strange and wonderful proverbs. Many have come down from the old Irish and are simply translated whilst others are imports but ring true to life.

Below are a number of the local and more common ones.

Fools' names like fools' faces are always seen in public places.

The nearer to the church, the further from God.

Better born lucky than rich.

A burned child dreads the fire.

Better wear out shoes than sheets.

It's too late to lock the stable door when the steed is stolen.

You never miss the water till the well runs dry.

It's never too late to mend.

Patience is a virtue, possess it if you can. It's always in a woman but seldom in a man.

Speak the truth and shame the Devil.

He who rises late had to trot all day.

Better wear out than rust out.

Two in distress makes sorrow less.

Where ignorance is bliss it's folly to be wise.

Light strokes fell great oaks.

The hole in the coat shows an empty pocket.

When wine is in wit is out.

Of two evils choose the least.

It's a long lane that has no turning.

The face that never wears a frown is lovelier than a velvet gown.
Empty vessels make most sound.

Take the world as it is, not as it ought to be.

Man proposes and god disposes.

A man's best friends are in his purse.

A fool and his money are soon parted.

When Poverty comes in at the door, love leaps out at the window.

Good to begin well, better to end well.

Beware of a silent man and a dog that does not bark.

Speech is silver, silence is golden.

Kind words are worth much and cost little.

No morning sun lasts a whole day.

A whistling woman and a crowing hen chose the Devil out of his den.

Better go to bed supper-less than rise in debt.

As the old cock crows the young one learns.

A green Christmas makes a fat graveyard.

Never bid the Devil good morrow till you meet him.

A man with learning and wearing bad clothes is highly respected wherever he goes.

Come day, go day. God sent Sunday.

Young a gambler, old a beggar.

Last time will never come back.

He who slings mud is losing ground.

Liars ought to have good memory.

Set a beggar on horseback and he will outride the Devil.

The longest way round is the nearest way home.

Music has charms to soothe the wild beasts.

A half nut can be divided.

After a storm there comes a calm.

What's allotted can't be blotted.

Ill got, ill gone.

Cut according to your cloth.

New Kings, new laws.

It is too late to spare when all is spent.

A constant drop wears a hole in a stone.

A going foot lifts a thorn.

Never too good to be your own servant.

Don't sell your chickens on a wet day.

Hard work never was easy.

Those who hide, find.

Self praise is no praise.

LUCKY DAYS

Of all days of the week, Friday has long been considered the unluckiest on which to be born or to get married. On the other hand, Friday is also thought to be lucky for many other things, such as beginning a new building project, taking up a new situation, going into a new house, or buying new stock.

Tuesday was considered a 'stormy day'. Anybody born on a Tuesday was said to have a hard life ahead, with obstacles to overcome. On no account would anyone ever go on a journey on a Tuesday.

People did not like to make changes of any kind on Thursday, though people born on a Thursday were born with a silver spoon in their mouth, which meant that they would always have plenty of money.

Sunday was considered a lucky day for anything – especially marriage – and people born on a Sunday always see the sunny side of things.

8

FOOLISHNESS

BILLY THE *AMADÁN*

There was once an old woman, a greedy aul' wench it has to be said, and she lived not far outside the village of Dowra with her grown-up son, Billy. Now Billy was a bit lacking in the brains department, and the unsympathetic people of the area used to call him Billy the *Amadán*.

They were very poor and barely had two shillings to rub together between them. The only thing of value they had was a single, solitary cow. One day when things were particularly tight, the old woman sent Billy to the village on fair day to sell the cow. She gave Billy strict instructions to ask for four pounds for the cow, but she also told him not to take the first or second bid but to take the third bid.

Billy then went along to the fair. There, a man came to him and said, 'How much do you want for the cow?'

'Four pounds,' said Billy.

'I'll give you three,' replied the man.

Billy then said to the man, 'My mammy told me not to take the first or second bid, but to take the third bid.' Hearing this, the man then offered him a sixpenny loaf. As this was the third bid, Billy accepted it and, on taking the loaf, gave the cow to the man.

Billy then proceeded home, quite happy with himself. As the road home was long, he got hungry and couldn't help himself; he ate half the loaf. Further along the road, he saw a poor aul' horse lying down and inches from death with hunger. Feeling sorry for the creature, he put the other half of the loaf into its mouth and went home.

When he reached home, his mother asked him how much he got for the cow. Billy told her the whole story, and she flew into a blind rage, hitting him with whatever she could lay her hands on. After some hours, she calmed down, and sent Billy out with a fine woven blanket to pawn to get some food to fill their bellies.

He set out later that evening and was back on the road to Dowra when the wind began to pick up and the heavens opened, pounding the earth with torrents of rain. He ran from hedge to hedge for cover until he finally came by a lone bush under which he was able to get some proper shelter from the elements. Billy was not long under the bush when the rainwater began to seep down through the branches and drop onto his head. He thought that the bush was crying with the cold and so, being the selfless whippet that he was, he spread the blanket out and put it over the top of the bush to keep it warm. He then went back home.

His mother asked him how he got on in the village and how much he got for the blanket. He told her his story and about the poor cold bush and the good deed he had done in keeping it warm. She got her blackthorn and, swinging wildly, hunted him out of the house with strict orders to go back and get the blanket. Billy went to the bush but the blanket was not there anymore.

Poor Billy was a little confused, got hold of a stick, and began beating the bush and asking it to give him back the blanket. The bush would not give it back to him. Knowing that he could not return home without it, he kept beating it until he started reducing it in size, and finally cut it down to the roots. There he saw a lot of shiny yellow things. He put some of them into his pocket and returned home, where his mother asked him where the blanket was. He told her that the bush would not give it to him and that he cut it down to the roots with a stick. 'But mammy,' he said, 'I got these nice things at the roots.'

When his mother saw what he had, and knowing that they were not mere 'shiny things', she asked him if there were any more in it. 'There are a lot more,' said Billy. 'Come and show me,' said his mother. Billy's mother filled her apron with the gold and they came home. She put the gold into a big chest in the parlour and told Billy not to tell a sinner about their hoard, but Billy told everyone anyway.

On hearing of their windfall, the local minister came looking for his half of the gold, and the old woman took him to the parlour and told him to take all the gold that he wanted. When he lent over and stooped into the chest to get the gold, she caught him by the feet and pushed him head first into the chest, closing the lid tight, and smothering him – the vile wench that she was.

She knew Billy would tell everyone, so she got up that night and dug a hole out on the bog in which she would bury the dead body of the minister but she got Billy involved and told him that she was too frail to bury the corpse herself, so he helped her. When the corpse was buried and Billy went to bed, she then took up the body and replaced it with an old dead goat instead.

It was not long before the police were out scouring the countryside in search of the minister, and when they met Billy on the road, he told them straight away of the fairy gold and his mammy's role in smothering and burying the poor old holy man out on the bog.

They asked Billy to dig where the body had been put, so he brought a spade from the house and started lifting the fresh earth.

He was not long digging when he came across the goat's horns, and became horrified. He cried, 'The minister must have turned into a devil since he went into the hole!' With that, he threw away the spade and ran home.

The police resigned themselves to the belief that Billy was making a fool of them, and they said, 'what would you expect from Billy the *Amadán*.'

THREE CONFUSED BUTTERMAIDS

One upon a time, there lived three women who could speak not one word of the King's English. They spoke only Irish from dawn to dusk and beyond.

The three ladies were farmers' wives and occasionally they went into the town to sell the butter that they had made on the farm. It was English that was spoken in town and nothing else, so they went to a man in their townland who knew both English and Irish. They asked him in Irish what they would say in English when they went to town, so he told them that they would be asked, 'How much do you want for the butter?' and they were to respond with 'Nine pence'. He went on to tell them that they would then be asked ,'Who made it?' and they were to respond with, 'We three.' The buyer would then say, 'I cannot take it,' and in reply to this, they were to say, 'If you don't, somebody else will.'

They started off on their journey, but little did they know that on the very same day, a murder was committed on the same road on which they were travelling. After the women had passed the place where the murder occurred, they met a detective and he said to them in English, 'Do you know anything about the murder, ladies?' to which they replied, 'Nine pence.' The detective said, 'You all must be mad', and so let them pass on. They continued on the road but met another detective and he asked the same question as the first. They replied, 'We three.' The detective said that he would have to summon them and they responded with, 'If you don't, somebody else will.' So he arrested them and had them detained in the police barracks. They were scheduled for a flogging the next day, but the man from their townland went and explained everything and they were then released, God be good to them.

WILLY THE FOOL

There once lived an old married couple in Castlerahan, a long, long time ago. The man was called Willy and the woman was called Milly. Now Willy was a bit soft and a bit senseless, but totally harmless. Milly, on the other hand, was the opposite. She was smart and short, intelligent but impatient.

Milly had gotten to the end of her tether with poor aul' Willy. The years of foolish chatter had worn her down and she had grown fierce tired of entertaining his constant nonsense.

One winter's evening a heavy storm was raging across the land, and Willy was cycling home from his job in the local abattoir. The torrents of rain and the sideways gusts of wind sent a shiver across Willy's back and a panic had come over him, for he was thinking what would happen if the weather became too much for their little house.

He frantically cycled *ar nós na gaoithe* and, jumping off his bike, he banged furiously on the wee timber door of their house, shouting 'Milly! Milly! Milly! Are you ok?' She opened the door and snapped at him, 'What ails you now, you old fool?' He pushed by his wife, and sat down beside the fireplace in the parlour and took off his wet socks to dry them over the hearth. He explained, 'I got to thinkin', Milly, what with that fierce blizzard blowing outside, what would we be doing if we had a wee *gosoon* in a crib here if the roof fell in on it?' With this, he began to break down and blubber over the thought of it all. I can tell you for sure that what Milly said next could not be printed in such a family book as this, so I will recount you with the abridged version.

Milly turned to him and, trying to keep a lid on her simmering rage, said, ''tis an *amadán* you are, Willy, as sure as I'm standing here. An *amadán* indeed. We have been married for over thirty long years and on the day my Daddy agreed to give my hand to you was the day he made the biggest mistake of his life.' Harsh words indeed from her, but she did not stop there. 'I have had enough of you, you old fool, and I am not going to stay with you any longer. In the morning at the first cock's crow, I shall be leaving this house and if I do not find three more people as foolish as you, then I shall not be returning to you or to this house ever again.'

So the next morning came and Willy heard the front door opening and closing just as the cock crew his first. He knew what this meant, and so it was that Milly had left and set out on the road for to find three fools comparable with her husband.

It was only in the next townland that Milly came across a young lad trying to get a wee donkey to climb a ladder onto the thatched roof of his house to eat the tufts of grass that grew out of the chimney. 'What are you trying to do there, lad?' said Milly to the young man.

'Sure, amen't I only trying to get the donkey up there to eat the grass there out of the chimney.'

''Tis only a fool you are,' said she in her usual curt fashion. She got up on the ladder and, climbing onto the roof, she pulled the tufts of grass out of the chimney and came back down, giving them to the donkey to eat. She said to the young lad, 'A fool like you is too stupid to own such a beast. This donkey is now mine,' and with that she set back out on the road with donkey in tow.

A little further on the road in the next parish, she passed a field with an old woman trying to give her horse some water to drink. She had her horse on one side of the road and a bucket of water on the other side. The woman would lift up the water from the bucket with her cupped hands and rush over to give it to the horse, but of course lost most of it on the way. 'What is it you are doing there, missus?' Milly asked. She was confused and thought to herself that the place was abundant with fools. She lifted up the bucket and brought it to the horse for to drink from. She said nothing (for once!) and continued on her journey with her donkey, that she had since named Willy, after her ass of a husband – yes, our Milly took no prisoners.

Milly had been travelling all day and she could feel the hunger pangs. She saw that the sun was beginning to set and knew that she had better look for somewhere to fill her belly and set her head before it got too late.

She saw a little cottage on the side of the road and went in to see an old woman, who was trying to light the fire. The old woman turned around and got a fright. 'Begorrah!' she let out in shock. 'Where did you come from?' Milly, wanting to have some fun with the poor old woman replied, 'Sure didn't I come from heaven itself.' The old woman asked her if she had seen her poor husband, who died some years back. 'Aye,' said Milly. 'I have seen your husband, and still fierce fond of the whiskey he is.'

'That's my Paddy,' said the old woman.

'Poor Paddy suffers something bad from the cold sometimes,' said Milly.

'Will you be going back to heaven anytime soon?' enquired the woman.

'Aye, I'll be going tomorrow but need something to eat and somewhere to rest my head beforehand.' The old woman gave Milly her own bed for the night whilst she was left to sleep on the cold flags. She settled down for the night and just before falling asleep thought to herself, 'Aren't there just a good many queer ones in this side of the country. The sooner one would get out of it all the better.'

On the first cock crow the following day, Milly got up and, after having a fine feed at the expense of the poor woman, set out on the long road home. She got home and knocked on the door of their little house. Her husband, Willy, opened the door and she embraced him, saying 'Sure, amen't I just lucky to have yourself, you old fool. I will never tire of listening to you again.' Milly knew from that day that there were a quite few creatures outside their home who were greater fools than her own Willy.

THE FOOLISH PAIR

Long ago there lived an old man and his wife in the townland. Their names were Jos and Biddy. They were very poor, because they had but one cow, and after some time the poor animal died, leaving them with no means of subsistence. They were much grieved at their loss, so one day Jos set out to earn some money. On the road, he met a fairy who told him what to do to find his fortune and although he thought it was strange, Jos carried out the instructions anyway. He told Biddy to cut the cow into small pieces and to leave a piece on every head of cabbage in their garden. Biddy went out to do as she was ordered, so she cut the cow in pieces and left a piece on every head of cabbage. That night, dogs ate all the meat and in the morning Jos lamented that they were worse off now than ever before. They faced for the road to beg and Jos told Biddy to pull the door after her. She was so foolish that she took the door on her back.

After a time they reached a wood and they heard a noise. Jos told Biddy to keep very still and that they would climb on to a bush. Biddy brought the door up also and they remained very still above. They heard another noise and saw a party of robbers come along and settled under the bush. They spread out a great quantity of food and whiskey and started to eat and drink. They then started counting all the money they had stolen. Biddy got so excited that she let the door leaf fall from the bush and the robbers, thinking it was a shot of a gun, ran away and left all behind them. Jos and Biddy got all the money and went home content. They never wanted for anything again.

9

CAUTIONARY TALES

THE CURSING STONES

Killinagh is a remote and foreboding place. Situated in the townland of Termon on the shores of the mysterious Lough MacNean in the east of the county, the several curious stone arrangements that poke through the rough and uneven surface here point to a dark past.

The medieval church, with its adjacent holy well of Toberbride and ruined megalithic tombs are a palpable reminder of the tolerant but uneasy marriage between the two great belief systems of the time – the native pagan nature worshippers versus the early Christian missionaries; the pagan Goddess of Brighid versus the early Christian St Brigid.

Nowhere is this relationship more evident than the three large glacial boulders to the north, on the banks of the lough. On the surface of each are large carved depressions known as *bullauns*, or rock basins. In each *bullaun* sits a perfectly rounded stone with a dark purpose. These are the famous Cursing Stones of St Brigid. When someone bore a grudge against a neighbour and wished them harm, they would visit the stones and perform a ritual to have the enemy anathematised or cursed. This act had grave risks for both the performer and the victim of the curse, which will

become clear. None learned this lesson better than young Molly Sheridan from nearby Blacklion in the townland of Tuam.

Molly was a sweet, young girl in her prime, yearning for nothing more than to be a wife and a mother. Molly had a soft spot for – and more than one romantic encounter with – a strapping young lad by the name of John Henry from just across the river in Belcoo in County Fermanagh. John loved nothing more than the hunt, and used to sneak away after a fine day in pursuit of the fox to see Molly. Although Molly fervently disapproved of John's penchant at killing poor defenceless creatures, she tolerated it as she loved him so.

There was a large hurdle that prevented their happiness, and this was their faith: John was Protestant and Molly was Catholic. Although this was usually a difficult but not an insurmountable barrier, the local rector in Belcoo made it impossible by forbidding any mixed marriages whatsoever.

Night after night the couple met in secrecy at the old Eel Weir that spanned the river and joined the two lands.

Desperate and frustrated, Molly lay awake that night thinking about their hopeless situation and what they could do to be together. She thought and thought when it finally came to her: surely St Brigid would help her?

She rose before sunrise early the next day and, being careful not to be seen by anybody, she traipsed across country and bog to the old church at Killinagh, arriving just as the mist was burned off the lake by the rising sun. Knowing the stories of what is said to reside at Killinagh, she quickly rounded the church, said a prayer at the Holy Well and, terrified and shaking, approached the Cursing Stones.

One by one, she turned the stones in their hollows against the sun, in an anti-clockwise direction, and prayed to St Brigid to curse the rector of Belcoo. She then took an old penny from her petticoat and placed it under the last stone for the fairies that live in the many forts that dot the hills around this place.

She quickly returned home, again being careful not to be seen by anybody and not telling anybody what she had done. She got into bed and arose again shortly after her family had got up so as not to arouse suspicion.

All day she thought about what she had done, and quickly the fear and worry in her grew, as she knew deep down that she had performed an act against her people and God. She knew that something bad was coming for her, as it is told that an unjust curse placed in the morning would rebound thricefold by nightfall. Molly went to bed early that night hoping to avoid any reprocussions.

She awoke refreshed the next day and stepping out of bed, she fell to the floor … on all fours. She began to panic and howl and, looking in the mirror, saw that she had been transformed into a fox. The noise had attracted the attention of her father, who burst into the room and began hitting Molly with a broom, not knowing what had happened. Molly ran out the door and towards the Belcoo river, looking for her beloved John to help.

She yelped and cried all the way until she got to the Eel Weir. Just then she saw her sweetheart on horseback galloping towards her. Her initial expression of joy quickly turned to terror when John blew his horn and she heard the beagles barking. This was the hunt, and she was the hunted. She turned around and ran as fast as she could, across ditches, bogs and fields, until she entered the old fairy fort at Tuam. She tried to scramble up the high banks on the other side, but kept slipping back down. In sheer dread, she realised that she was trapped; hearing the dogs' barking getting louder and closer, she could only wait for the inevitable. Cowering under a branch, the beagles grabbed hold of her, and she saw her beloved John raise the baton high above his head and bring it down forcibly upon her head, cracking her skull and killing her instantly.

CILLIAN OF MULLAGH AND KILIAN OF WÜRZBURG

One of the greatest frontier men and pioneers to have come out of the area now occupied by the county was that of our very own Cillian.

Born into the ruling nobility of the Gailenga in the seventh century in the area around Cloughballybeg, not a stone's throw from the wee hamlet of Mullagh, our pioneer of piety recognised God's calling from a very young age. Renouncing his royal duties, he travelled to Roscarbery in the south west of the island to commence his studies as a novice monk.

During this time of learning, it became apparent to all that Cillian was destined for great things, surpassing all that was expected of him at every turn, as he did. On completion of his training, he set up a monastery in Kenmare, and trained many of his contemporaries there.

Deciding that it was time to spread the word to farther flung places, he set out in a *currach* with twelve of his most trusted companions and, braving the ferocious elements of wind and sea, arrived some months later in Rome seeking orders from the Pope. Pope Conan directed them to Germany and more specifically to the province of Franconia, where they set up their headquarters at Würzburg. Everywhere he went, Cillian could see the local peoples engaged in the acts of pagan and nature worship; acts that were contrary to the Christian beliefs he had come to accept as true.

His message of peace and reconciliation was received with open arms by many, and in a very short time he was received by

Duke Gosbert, ruler of the locality, who was so impressed with his message that he converted to Christianity.

Some years later a scandal erupted in the province and, to Cillian's disappointment, it was discovered that the duke was having an affair with his brother's wife, Geilana. Cillian immediately denounced and condemned the goings on, much to Geilana's fury.

The old quote 'Hell hath no fury like a woman scorned' rings very true in this case. It was on the following day that Cillian and his two companions, Colman and Totnan, were kneeling in prayer in the town square when two assassins under the orders of the vile Geilana set upon them. They were ferociously beaten where they knelt in communication with God, and their heads were then brutally sliced from their bodies and their corpses unceremoniously buried.

Such was the abhorrence of the Franconians of such an act that the three hallowed heads were enshrined and kept as sacred relics in Würzburg Castle, where they are kept to this day, being brought out on his feast day every year.

Cillian is celebrated in his home town, at the Holy Well he created, and those suffering from the affliction of rheumatism seek relief at this place.

The Kilianstein

Atop a hill beside the town of Winterstein in the Sembach Valley of central Germany exists a strange rock tower, unlike anything else in the neighbouring countryside. It rises 500 metres above sea level and is comprised of quartz porphyry stone.

It was at this place many years ago during the time of Cillian's mission to the area at the behest of Pope Conon that he was involved in his godly duties of converting the masses to Christianity. The majority of people warmed to Cillian and his friends so much that their conversion was an easy task for the saints.

Less pleased with the arrival of Cillian was the Devil, who, on hearing of the good work that was happening, became furious. In passing through the valley, he rammed his staff into the earth in anger and frustration at the saints' success. In removing his staff from the ground, the tip remained lodged there and this has been known as The Kilianstein or Cillian Stone ever since.

RICH BROTHER, POOR BROTHER

There were once two brothers who lived in two separate cabins on opposite ends of the same farm. One of them was rich and the other was poor. The rich man hated his poor brother because he was always scrounging money from him. In fact, the rich brother hated the poor brother to such an extent that he made up his mind for to kill him. There is no doubt that money makes people do crazy things.

The next time the poor man went to his brother's cabin, didn't the rich brother take the poker from the hearth and beat him unmercifully. If this weren't punishment enough, the rich brother got the tongs and pulled out his poor brother's eyes, then threw him into a limekiln, leaving him there to die.

As can be imagined, the poor man was suffering very much with the shock and pain of it all. Just after twelve o'clock in the night, he heard the cats crying and realised that a whole army of them had gathered outside and all around the kiln. Passing the time before he expired and to take his mind off the fierce pain he was in, the poor man asked each of them to tell a story; the black tabby replied that they would tell a story but only if there was nobody else around to listen.

All the cats searched around the farm but they could find nobody, so being assured that there was nobody listening, the black tabby began to tell the story. He told of the great old ash tree that grew nearby, where water collected within a fork in its branches. This water was magic and had the cure for all sicknesses and injuries, particularly those of sore eyes. When the cats went away, the man crawled out of the kiln and felt around for the tree and the magic water that he heard the tabby tell of. He eventually found it, and rubbed some on his eyes and drank the rest. Not only were his eyes restored but he also felt quite strong and well again.

He went back to the kiln the next night to hear what the cats would have to tell. The cats did the same as the night before and could not find anybody, so one of the cats began to tell a story. She told the others where there was a hill with gold and silver in it. After the cats went away, the man went and found the gold. Then he went home and bought clothes for his wife and family.

The rich brother wondered how his poor brother recovered so well after the fierce pulverising he gave him, as well as how he had gotten so rich, so he went and asked him to tell him the secret. The brother who was poor at first told his brother about the cats and their tales. The rich man also went to the kiln the following night and when the cats came along, they searched to see if anyone was there. They found the rich man, tore him to pieces, killing him.

I can't say that I feel too bad for the rich brother.

An Féar Gortach Agus An Fóidín Mearbhaill

It is well known by the country folk that there are certain places you can walk and there are certain places you cannot.

This story is about two such places, famed in folklore and well known in many places around the island. Tales of these places occur at many points in our history, but given the many recorded accounts of those succumbing to their perils, the dangers clearly still remain unknown to many.

The Hungry Grass

The Hungry Grass, or *An Féar Gorta* (sometimes also called Fairy Grass), is a type of crab grass, not easily identifiable or discernible from the other type to the naked eye. It is said that at the places where it grows lie the corpses of those unfortunates who died during the potato famine of the 1840s. It is rumoured that the strength of the unwary traveller is sucked away by the hungry bones that lie beneath.

Knowing where these grasses grew was imperative for the health and welfare of the people, and it was custom in many places to sprinkle the grass with leftover crumbs from the table in order to stave off the Hungry Grass and stop it spreading. Many a smart person would be sure to have a biscuit or piece of bread in their pocket when taking a stroll out in the countryside, as if captured by the hungry grass, an insatiable hunger will come upon you. If a morsel of food is not ingested (that's all it takes), then the risk of immediate death is high.

The Stray Sod

It is believed that all around the county are stray sods, sites cursed by the wee people. Known in the Irish as *An Fóidín Mearbhaill*, they are a danger to those out and about in the evening who unknowingly stand on such a sod. The unwary traveller loses all sense of direction and his bearings leave him entirely, even though he may have known where he was a moment previously. The poor sod (pardon the pun) is left to wander hopelessly around full of confusion, and generally until morning.

It is helpful if such a thing happens to you to take off your coat and turn it inside out and wear it thus. That is the only hope of undoing the charm.

Tom McGeehan of Redhills, near Belturbet, was out checking on his cattle one evening in the 1920s when he trod on a stray sod. He was not found for two days; when he was discovered, he was found aimlessly wandering near Porton, some 16 Irish miles away. He was never quite right after that.

HARVEY'S TREASURE

In olden times, when there were no banks at all in Ireland, it was not unusual for people to hide money and precious things in strange and unusual places, such as in graveyards and on the banks of rivers. I have often heard stories of people drowning or dying before they had a chance to retrieve their precious treasure and their goods lying unclaimed for many years.

In former times, about a hundred yards from Cornacrum school, was a small farmhouse. In this house there lived a man and woman by the name of Harvey, along with their servant boy, who returned to his own home in the evenings.

Harvey was well to do and had a fair bit of land around the area to his name. He did well from his farm, but worked hard for every shilling he got. He kept the money he earned in a cloth bag buried in the dirt floor of the barn. He was also a very hospitable man and people came from miles around to stay at his house for the night before a fair, where they were always welcome to a fine supper and a firm bed.

One day, news reached Harvey that a famous highwayman was carrying out robberies in the locality, so he made up his mind that his normal hiding place was not good enough and that he would have to find another safe spot for his gold. He took his kit from behind the kitchen door and went up to the barn for to dig up the bag of money. He went out over the bog and planned to bury it near the old *sceach* on the bog but, on climbing over the fence, didn't he trip. With this, the bag flew out of his hand and into a bog hole. The poor man frantically searched for his money and prized possessions, but they were all gone then and have not been seen since.

Poor Mr Harvey is long since dead and so is everybody who ever knew him. It is said that one day someone will get a nice surprise when out digging the turf.

LAKE OF THE PHYSICIAN

The townland boundaries of Bracklin and Mohercrom run directly through the centre of Loughanleagh, these days now barely a shadow of its former self, with it being no more than a damp depression within a modern conifer plantation. Known as *Lough an Liagha* in the old tongue, meaning Lake of the Physician or Lake of Cures, it was believed that the rules of the world did not apply to it or to its behaviour.

Said to have been a doorway to the fairy realm, no direct source for the water and stream from the lough could be found. Its quality always remained sweet and fresh to drink, whilst its level and temperature never once fluctuated. Those afflicted with various ailments sought and obtained cures in its magical waters and in its sacred mud.

On the eve of every *Lúnasa* in the old calendar, a large supernatural hare would rise from the lough and go bounding across the mountain tops from cairn to cairn, lighting the way with the large glowing red eye that protruded from its forehead.

Before the sun rose on the following morning, the hare would return to the lough and, with a single leap, jump into the centre and disappear into the murky depths back to the Otherworld.

A certain high-ranking army man of means from Kingscourt, being of a particular persuasion, had little time for the old ways. He vowed to put an end to what he deemed to be the folly of the lough. Saying, 'I'll show the country people the folly of their beliefs,' he transported his diseased hounds out to the lough and forcibly drove them into the water.

Although they shrieked and whimpered in fear, he only allowed them out after a few moments. Miraculously, they had received the cure from the waters and no longer suffered from the mange; however, the deliberate offence caused by the major resulted in the lough losing its sacredness and power to heal.

Not being satisfied with the damage he had already done, he knew of the supernatural hare's habits. 'In for a penny, in for a pound,' said he, and in a gross act of wanton vandalism, got his workmen to plant conifers all around the banks of the water and across the hillside. He knew that when these trees grew bigger that they would choke the lough, drain it of all its life-giving water, and in the process close off the doorway to the Otherworld.

Sadly, nobody goes to Loughanleagh for the cure anymore, nor has the poor one-eyed hare been seen around Bracklin or Mohercrom. Oh, and the major? Well, on returning home, he tripped and lost his footing, falling head first into the kennel where his hounds sat. Given that they were no longer ill, they all had fine appetites. The major's bones were found some three days later, licked clean and with not a bit of meat left on them.

THE TURF CUTTER'S WAKE

Once upon a time there lived a man name Martin Doyle over in nearby Belturbet. He was married and had a sister living in County Dublin. Every day he brought a creel of turf from the bog convenient to his house. On the way to the bog, he had to cross a flooded ditch; as there was no bridge over it, he had to walk on a plank of wood.

At that time, there was no postal service in Ireland and the majority of people had no education – many of them were not able to read or write. When a person would write to their friends, they had to send a messenger with it. One day, Martin's sister wrote to him and sent a messenger from County Dublin with it. When he landed, he asked his wife where Doyle was and she told him that he was out on the bog for a creel of turf, and so the messenger went to meet him.

Martin had just got the creel filled when he got the letter from the messenger. When Doyle read the letter, he found out that his sister was sick and that she had asked him to come to Dublin and see her. Martin said to the messenger that he could not go because he had no clothes except ragged ones and that he had a five pound note at home but he would not waste any time in buying any. The Dublin man had a fine suit of clothes on him and Doyle asked him if he would give him the suit of clothes; he would give him his old clothes and the five pound note in exchange. The messenger duly agreed and so they changed clothes right there, out on the bog.

Then Doyle set out on his journey to Dublin but before leaving, he put the load of turf on the messenger and asked him to take it to the house. Unfortunately, on the way, the messenger fell off the plank into the ditch. As the Dublin man was not used to carrying a creel, he did not know how to unfasten himself from it. At nightfall, Martin's wife told the neighbours to search for Martin in the bog and they found the messenger drowned in the ditch. They brought the body home, believing that it was Martin they had with them. The messenger was waked and buried, and Martin did not know anything that happened.

Martin's sister died and she left Martin a great token of money, with which he returned home. It was Christmas Eve night when he landed; when he knocked on the door, his wife asked him who he was.

He said he was Martin, but his wife would not let him into the house. She thought that it was her Martin who had died, and hadn't she only gotten married again? Martin slept in a stall that night and he went to first Mass Christmas morning. The people frightened when they saw him coming and thought it was his ghost. When Martin arrived at the chapel, all the people were frightened and rushed towards the altar.

The priest enquired what had happened, but when Martin told the priest his story, the priest responded by informing Martin of his death and burial; however, it was concluded that instead of Martin being buried, it was the messenger. The priest told Martin that his wife was married again and if he wished, he could hunt the other man, but Martin replied that he would live by himself. The priest explained the story to the congregation and told them that it was Martin Doyle that they had seen and not his ghost.

THE OFFENDED WELL

Wells and springs have been held sacred by the Irish since time immemorial. These natural places, which are to be found all over the country, have sustained local peoples both physically and spiritually from before the time of the druids to the present day.

Many Holy Wells are located in areas of natural beauty, often in groves of trees, hollows in the landscape, the edge of waysides, or at points where borders and boundaries run or meet. Others are hidden in darkness in mysterious underground tunnels, chambers, or caves, and others again at the edge of the sea, where the salt water mixes with their own twice each day.

The waters of Holy Wells are associated with the power of divination and the cure of specific or general disorders. It is believed that this power is strongest on the Pattern Day, usually a significant date on the Pagan and/or Christian calendar and different for each well. A certain ritual, known as a 'round' or 'station' is performed in order to receive a requested favour or cure of a particular ailment.

This involves particular prayers being said whilst walking around the well an odd number of times in the direction of the sun, and drinking or bathing in the waters at specific intervals. To complete the round, a rag, symbolising the ailment, is tied to the sacred 'rag tree', usually an ash, hawthorn, holly, or oak. If the round is completed in reverse in the name of a third party, a curse is placed on that person, but worse consequences are reputed to befall the person who performs such an act if it is not deserved. Realising their importance, the early saints took over as patrons and ensured that they remained respected as reverent special places.

There was an old woman called Biddy who lived at Coratinner and she was a wee bit difficult. She would sow the spuds the day before St Patrick's Day, which is against 'the way', eat eggs during Lent, and have fish for supper every day of the week but eat meat on Fridays. Yes, she was quite a pup.

One day, her neighbour called into Biddy on a Sunday morning for a cup of tea before heading up to the chapel for Mass, something that they had done together every Sunday morning for many years.

Having not gone to the pump the night before, she did not have enough water in the house to boil a kettle. Her friend said, 'Ah sure it's no bother, we can offer it up for our sins, and head along to Mass.' Not wanting to be beaten, Biddy insisted that she must have her tea so she told her neighbour that she would follow her on to the chapel. Biddy took the kettle and instead of going to the nearest pump, headed across the field to *Tobar Ultan*, the holy well.

She got there and, although knowing that what she was doing was forbidden, washed out the kettle in the sacred water and then filled it up. She carried it back home, deciding that she would not be bothered to go to Mass now and would instead put her feet up with a nice tea and relax. She put the kettle on the range and it started to boil away, but there was something not quite right. The lid started to lift off quite dramatically and a thick red substance began to ooze out. Biddy realised that this was not water, but blood!

She shrieked in horror and, realising that she had really gone too far this time, grabbed the kettle and ran out of the house. She turned in the direction of the well and ran as quickly as she could until she got to the edge. She turned the kettle upside down and released the liquid back into the well; no longer was it blood, but water once again.

Biddy vowed to mend her ways and even became caretaker of the well.

THE POOR LAD AND THE EVIL STEPMOTHER

Once upon a time, there lived together a husband and his wife, as common a thing then as it is today. They had a son who was 6 years of age when his mother unfortunately passed away. About a year after this, his father married again.

The little boy was so nice that everybody admired him for his beauty, God be good to him. The stepmother was not long in the house when the people noticed the little boy failing and it was no wonder as the stepmother was very cruel to him. She used to beat him and would not give him a bit to eat bar a grain of meal that she would place on the flag floor in the mornings and the same at night. If this were not bad enough, she would not give him a spoon but would insist that he lick it off the floor.

In his father's presence, she pretended to be very fond and good to him, but she would always make sure to have him in bed before the father came home from work. The father would often ask why she did not have the little lad up when he came home from work, but she always said that the young boy was a bit pale and she thought it best for him to be in bed early.

One night, the stepmother became very ill; she could not get out of bed and the doctor was sent for. The young boy was sitting on one side of the fire and the father on the other. The boy began to talk in Irish, as in those days nothing else was spoken. 'I wish my feet were washed, the flag was licked, and I was in bed.' The father looked confused and surprised; he asked, 'What do you mean by "the flag was licked"?' so the young boy told him that he had to lick meal off the flagstone floor every morning and every night and this was the only food he got. The father was in an awful state, and said, 'Why did you not tell me about this before?' The boy replied that his stepmother threatened to kill him if he said anything but he knew that now that she was sick, she could not touch him.

After the doctor left the house, the father went to her and told her that he had her found out and that she must leave the house immediately and return to her own people, for he would not bear her presence any longer for how she had been treating his son. He told her that the son was a fine healthy boy before she came to the house and that he now knew why he was so pale. The stepmother begged her husband to let her recover from her sickness in the house and then she would leave; he reluctantly agreed to this and when the time came she left.

Years rolled on and the father died from old age, as is the way of it. The boy grew up to be a man and got married and had a family of his own. One night, they were sitting around the fire and having their supper when they heard a knock on the door. The man opened the door and saw an old woman standing there, with her clothes all torn and her perished with the cold. She asked him if could she come in; the lad, being taught well by his father, brought her in, sat her at the fire, and gave her some supper.

After talking with them a long time, he realised that she was his stepmother. She told him that nobody would have her after her behaviour and asked for his forgiveness. The man forgave her and after her supper, she bade him farewell and went back out into the darkness.

Printed in Great Britain
by Amazon